The Glories and Wildness of North Wales

Exploring North Wales between 1810 and 1860 with
The Reverend John Parker

Rev. John Parker of Sweeney Hall by Charles Edward Halle, 1859

The Glories and Wildness of North Wales

Exploring north Wales between 1810 and 1860 with
the Reverend John Parker

Edward Parry

First published in: 2022
© Edward Parry/Gwasg Carreg Gwalch 2022

All rights reserved.
No part of this publication may be reproduced, stored in a retrieval system, or transmitted in any form or by any means, electronic, electrostatic, magnetic tape, mechanical, photocopying, recording, or otherwise, without prior permission of the authors of the works herein.

ISBN: 978-1-84527-845-8

Published with the financial support of the Books Council of Wales

CYNGOR LLYFRAU CYMRU
BOOKS COUNCIL of WALES

Cover and layout design: Eleri Owen
Cover image: *Llyn y Gader between Beddgelert and Caernarvon, midday 1818*

All images by John Parker are reproduced by
Llyfrgell Genedlaethol Cymru /
The National Library of Wales permission copyright.

A note on the illustrations:
Unless indicated otherwise, all the paintings and drawings are by John Parker. Much of his work is not titled; where he provided a title it is shown in italics and inverted commas; the captions in regular type are by the author.

All photographs are by the author except for three on pages 68, 89, and 98.

Every effort has been made to contact owners and clear all possible copyright issues. If we have offended in any way, we express our sincerest regret.

Published by Gwasg Carreg Gwalch,
12 Iard yr Orsaf, Llanrwst, Wales LL26 0EH.
tel: 01492 642031
e-mail: books@carreg-gwalch.cymru
website: www.carreg-gwalch.cymru

Printed and published in Wales.

For my grandchildren
Pippa Edith and Percy Glyn

Preface

John Parker is little known today, even in the part of Wales where he spent all his life. Mention the name and antiquarians and architectural historians would assume you were referring to John Henry Parker, a much better known contemporary, the author of *An Introduction to the study of Gothic Architecture* (1849) and later Keeper of the Ashmolean Museum at Oxford. Had the two Parkers met they would have enjoyed animated discussions about medieval buildings and the evolution of the Gothic style.

'My' John Parker enjoyed little of the renown of his namesake, living as a modest country clergyman in two secluded parishes close to the Welsh border. But at the National Library of Wales, in Aberystwyth, there is a Parker archive of journals and drawing volumes which shows him to have been not only a perceptive recorder of his many journeys throughout Britain – to Snowdonia in particular – but also an accomplished and prolific artist. What he wrote and drew has rarely seen the light of day since his death in 1860; little use has been made of what is a wonderful source of information about Wales in the first half of the nineteenth-century. *The Glories and Wildness of North Wales* – Parker's description of Snowdonia – aims to demonstrate in his own words, complemented by his paintings, why John Parker deserves to be rescued from obscurity.

Edward Parry

Contents

Introduction 9

1 Early years, 1798–1827 11

2 Parker the Anglican clergyman 19

3 The Passengers 29

4 The Picturesque and the 'discovery' of North Wales 33

5 Parker's journeys to North Wales 41

6 Walking with Parker 55

7 Exploring the landscape 61

8 Parker the Artist 73

9 Parker and the buildings of North Wales 85

10 Parker the architect and builder 105

Conclusion 115

Postscript 116

Acknowledgements 118

Index 119

GOGLEDD/
NORTH
Beaumaris
Conwy
St Asaph
Bangor
The Menai Bridge
Llandygái
Llyn
Geirionydd
Llyn
Crafnant
Bethesda
Llyn Bychan
Llynnau
Mymbyr
Llanrwst
Llyn Peris
Caernarfon
Llanberis
Glyder
Fach
Tryfan
Gwydir
Capel Curig
Glyder
Fawr
Maen Du
Penygwryd
Betws-y-coed
Llyn Cwellyn
Snowdon
Llyn
Moel Siabod
Llyn
Elsi
The 'Irish Road'
Lliwedd
Llydaw
Rhaeadr y
Graig Lwyd
(Conwy Falls)
Clynnog
Fawr
Beddgelert
Y Cnicht
Valle Crucis
Abbey
Tre'r Ceiri
Ffestiniog
Pontcysyllte
aqueduct
Plas Tan-y-bwlch
Llangollen
Pwllheli
Bala
Rhiwaedog
Llyn Tegid
Harlech
Pistyll
Rhaeadr
Oswestry
Llanengan
Llansilin
Llangynog
Sweeney Hall
Aran
Fawddwy
Morton
Corsygedol
Nannau
Llanyblodwel
Ynys Enlli
Bodowen
Dolgellau
Barmouth
Cader Idris
Craig y Deryn
('bird rock')
Aberllefenni
Llanegryn
Peniarth
Machynlleth
Greenfields
0 milltir/miles 10
0 cilomedrau/kilometres 20
Yn cynnwys data'r Arolwg Ordnans
© Hawlfraint y Goron a hawl cronfa ddata 2022
Contains Ordnance Survey data
© Crown copyright and database right 2022
Newtown
Llanmerewig
Penarth

Introduction

In the summer of 1860, an elderly Anglican clergyman, his married sister and her daughter made what was in effect a pilgrimage to Snowdonia. The Reverend John Parker was 61 and in poor health but he had persuaded Mary, Lady Leighton, to accompany him on his last journey to the area that had captivated him since he was a schoolboy. His earliest surviving sketch is a pencil drawing signed 'J P near Lanberris' [sic] dated September 1810 and his last, the view from above the road east of Llanberis, done on 13 June 1860. In the intervening years, Parker made numerous visits to Snowdonia and to other parts of North Wales, and what he wrote and drew comprise one of the most complete records left by the hundreds of tourists who committed their impressions to diaries and sketchbooks.

Parker has also left accounts of his travels to Ireland, Scotland and one expedition to the Rhineland, northern Italy and France. His English journeys included visits to the Lakes, the Midlands and the South West. Parker explored parts of South Wales in 1831, 1836 and 1843 and made frequent visits to Radnorshire, particularly to inspect the screen at Llananno church. His drawing volumes contain beautiful watercolours of Tintern Abbey, St David's cathedral and Chepstow castle as well as detailed drawings of church interiors. However, it was Snowdonia that drew him back year after year and where he felt most in sympathy with the people and the landscape, which is why this book concentrates on his tours of North Wales.

While many contemporaries published accounts of journeys in Wales, Parker's venture into print does not do justice to his significance as an observer of the landscape and its inhabitants. *The Passengers* (1831) records an imagined journey from Oswestry to the summit of Snowdon, written in a very mannered style in the form of conversations between three friends. While it illustrates clearly Parker's twin passions for landscape and architecture, its didactic tone means it lacks the appeal of his journals. It has only two illustrations, a frontispiece showing an elaborately decorated Gothic entrance to a church and one black-and-white engraving. Attached to *The Passengers* is a long poem, 'The Celtic Annals', in which the author indulges in a romantic account of the history of Wales and its inhabitants from their origins in 'the sunburnt East … Where cloud-girt Ararat rose as a luminous island' to their subjugation by the Normans.

Unlike some tourists, whose accounts of their journeys are predictably similar and rather hackneyed, Parker wrote well, with fluency and a gift for description and anecdote. He also at times used his writings to unburden himself of anxieties and to indulge in self-reflection, which make them more personal than many travellers' memoirs. His landscapes capture vividly the shapes and colours of Snowdonia; he was also a meticulous draughtsman who recorded the details of buildings and church furnishings with an accuracy that makes them valuable records today. His extensive knowledge of the British Isles and parts of Western Europe enabled him to compare landscapes and buildings in Wales with those of other countries, usually to the advantage of Wales. His appreciation of Gothic architecture in particular was scholarly and based on years of careful examination of cathedrals and churches all over Britain. While the mountains captured his heart, Parker's mind was in thrall to architecture.

North Wales showing places visited by Parker

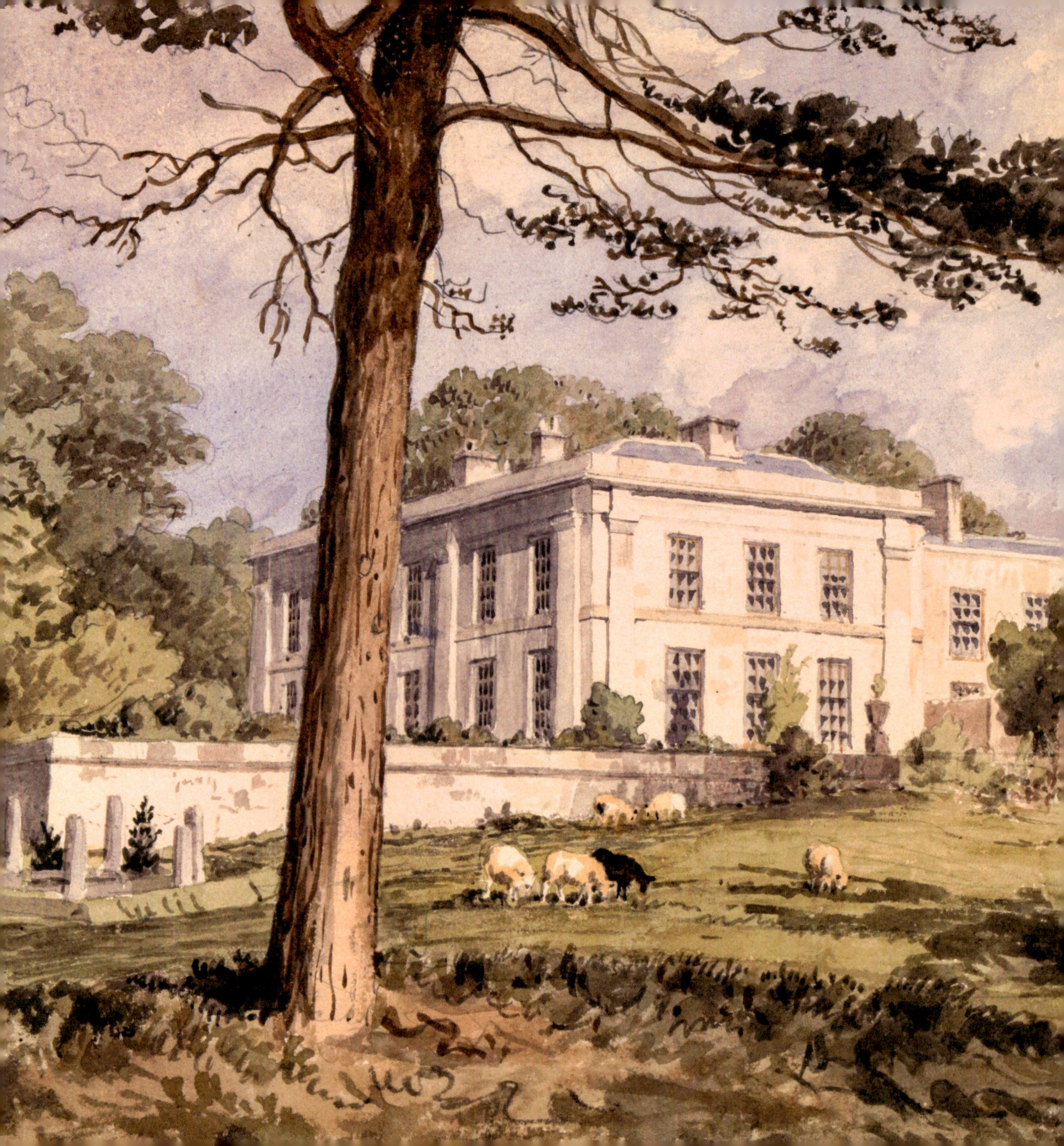

Chapter One
Early years, 1798–1827

John Parker's painting of Sweeney Hall
Now a hotel, Sweeney Hall is an early nineteenth-century country house with a classical frontage. The house stood in a fine park now bisected by the Oswestry by-pass, but with some fine trees still standing. The front portion of the house has changed little since he lived there.

John Parker was from a gentry family, the second son of Thomas Netherton Parker and Sarah Browne.[1] His father was a landowner in Worcestershire who, by his marriage in 1796 to Sarah, the heir of Edward Browne of Sweeney Hall, Oswestry, came to Shropshire. John is often described as of Sweeney Hall, but he was born in October 1798 at Hatton Grange, Shifnal, which his parents had leased just over a month earlier. The family moved to Sweeney Hall in 1816. He had an older brother, Thomas, and two younger sisters, Mary and Elizabeth, born between 1797 and 1802, of whom only Mary married. Thomas died in 1833 and John inherited the estate on his father's death in 1848, but it appears that his mother managed the property until she died in 1854. Failing health and his preoccupation with building projects in Llanyblodwel meant that John took little part in the business of the estate, which passed to his brother-in-law Sir Baldwin Leighton Bt of Loton Park in 1860.

Thomas Netherton Parker, who served as a magistrate and mayor of Oswestry, was a man of wide interests and played a prominent part in the affairs of his area. His many, eclectic publications included *Suggestions for Warming and Ventilating the Houses of Parliament with Hot Water in Cast-Iron Pipes*. He was also concerned with social problems and he produced *Plans, Specifications, Estimates and Remarks on Cottages... for Bettering the Conditions and Increasing the Comforts of the Poor*. In 1816, when the country was experiencing an economic depression following the end of the Napoleonic wars, he wrote a long letter to the London Association for the Relief of the Manufacturing and Labouring Poor advocating a scheme encouraging employers to take on extra labourers, as he himself did. Today, he is probably best known for the *Justice's Book*, his handwritten record of over a hundred cases which he heard at the petty sessions between 1805 and 1813. The manuscript shows a magistrate who encouraged those who appeared before him to settle their disagreements in an amicable fashion and to avoid if possible the legal process, and 'in a significant number of cases [he] exercised a considerable amount of judicial discretion.'[2] His father's example of a paternalistic landowner who took his social responsibilities seriously was one which made a lasting impression on his second son.

John followed his elder brother to Eton; he first appears on the college list in 1811. While he had ambivalent memories of his schooldays, at Eton he showed a talent for drawing and an interest in the architecture of historic buildings which were to preoccupy him as an adult. Among his contemporaries were two sons of John Luxmoore, Bishop of St Asaph; Charles, later the long-serving vicar of Guilsfield in Montgomeryshire and his elder brother John who became a canon

John Parker as a young man probably painted by his sister Mary. I am grateful to Sir Michael Leighton, Bt, for permission to reproduce it here.

Eton college and chapel

of St Asaph and rector of Marchwiel and married a Miss Pusey, the sister of another contemporary, Edward Bouverie Pusey. Two of his schoolfellows, Charles Luxmoore and Henry Neave, accompanied Parker on his early tours of North Wales.

Parker went up to Oriel college, Oxford, in 1816 and graduated in 1820 just as the college was experiencing a period of intellectual ferment, with Keble, Newman and Pusey among the Fellows, all influential in the Oxford Movement. The Movement's desire to re-establish the connections between the nineteenth-century church and its medieval heritage had a great appeal to Parker, particularly in architectural terms. In 1842, he joined the Cambridge Camden Society – the only Welsh incumbent to do so. Renamed the Ecclesiological Society in 1845, it became the most influential force in the country for the study and promotion of Gothic church architecture.

In almost everything he wrote, Parker comes across as a man of great enthusiasms who relished his travels

Eton contemporaries

and the opportunities they provided for seeing new places and meeting interesting people. On just a couple of occasions this sanguine mood deserts him and the writing becomes introspective and the travel journals become personal diaries. Such entries occur when he was a young man, in his twenties, before he accepted the living of Llanmyrewig in 1827.

John Parker was 22 when, in June 1820, he spent twelve days in Snowdonia and on the Mawddach estuary, at Bodowen, his uncle's house, and his journal contains some of his most elegiac comments on the countryside and its effects on his feelings: 'This last tour has left more splendid impressions upon my fancy than any other.' He relished the days in the mountains for another reason: 'the freedom from embarrassments as to university examination'. In his account of this tour, he mentions twice his fatigue, 'from the effects of former illness'. It is not clear whether there was any connection between his illness and his anxiety about examinations.[3]

In the summer of 1821 he returned to Bodowen. 'Wednesday 3rd October My birthday, this day I am twenty-three. If omens can be drawn from birthdays, the rest of my life will be wretched enough, for I rose at half past four in the morning and waited until 6 o'clock for the Barmouth coach, the day was completely rainy, and neither sun nor blue sky were to be seen anywhere.' Perhaps not too much importance should be attributed to a wet birthday; he had felt unwell earlier that week with a 'headache, sickness, tendency to fainting making me very uneasy'.

More significant is the much longer journal entry of August 1822 when he was staying at the Capel Curig inn and his ambivalent feelings towards his old school and university resurfaced. He climbed Moel Siabod and this brought back memories of his schooldays at Eton: 'the place where learning appeared to reside only by compulsion, and poetic feeling to be engulfed by mechanical blunders; much as I esteem public schools in general, there is a heartless, outward show of diligence about them injurious and undignified.' His time at the university was also recalled with mixed emotions. 'During my stay there from being almost loathsome to me, from appearing to be stained with endless vices'; yet he could also write, 'and thou O Oxford, once hated, now belov'd with what strange emotions do I recollect thee, with what regret? In thee misunderstanding and ill-usage made me wretched in thee also did I obtain thoughts, more precious to me than health or riches. In thee also did I meet with disappointment, yet I cannot now dislike thee.' Parker believed that since his time at Eton and Oriel 'rapid advances have been made, both in schools and at Oxford. I have past thro an university education at a time when English youth had begun to esteem wisdom and to pursue knowledge with real energy.' He ended this melancholy but affecting account with a prayer: 'Grant me cheerfulness and patience, O Creator, that I may await the time when purity of intention shall become apparent and the truth be acknowledged as well as error.'

Whatever was behind such confessions, the rest of his life seems to have passed without any emotional crises. He was very close to his sister Mary and on good terms with other members of his family. Many of his journeys began from Sweeney Hall and on some of his tours, notably the one to the Rhineland in 1827, he was accompanied by Mary and his mother.

Oriel College, Oxford

[1] The only previous account of Parker's life and travels is by Edgar W. Parry, *Revd John Parker's Tour of Wales and its Churches (1798-1860)*, 1998; this includes extensive extracts from his journals and a number of black-and-white illustrations, principally of churches. I found it a very useful introduction to the man and his work. The most comprehensive account of Parker's journeys is on Michael Freeman's website, *Early Tourists in Wales, 18th and 19th century tourists' comments about Wales. Edward Parry, The Revd John Parker: 'a warm partizan of Gothic art',* in the Transactions of the Ancient Monuments Society, volume 64, 2020, covers some of the same ground as the present book but concentrates on his architectural and antiquarian interests. There is a brief essay on Parker by M.A. Goodall in the *Oxford Dictionary of National Biography* (2004).

The National Library of Wales Journal (volume IV, numbers 1 & 2, 1945-6 pp. 90-91 and volume V, number 1, 1947-8, p.69) includes notes on the bequest by the Parker Leighton family of John Parker's drawings. Soon after the donation postcards of ten of Parker's paintings were reproduced, followed in 1950 by a travelling exhibition of some of his works. Since then Parker has largely disappeared from public view, although copies of his drawings of screens have appeared in scholarly articles in *Archaeologia Cambrensis* and in specialist books such as Richard Wheeler's *The Medieval Church Screens of the Southern Marches,* 2006, Logaston Press.

An exhibition in 2001 at the National Library of Wales with the Royal Cambrian Academy of Art, curated by Dr Paul Joyner, included two works by Parker. On the front cover of the catalogue Parker's watercolour shows the summit of Cader Idris at sunrise with representations of the mountain or Brocken spectre; the second a view of Llyn y Cau on Cader Idris dated 1840. (I am grateful to Peter Bishop for drawing my attention to this source.)

The latest volume from the Royal Commission on the Ancient and Historical Monuments of Wales, *Painted Temples: Wallpaintings and Rood-screens in Welsh Churches, 1200-1800* by Richard Suggett, 2021 includes some of Parker's drawings of churches and their furnishings.

[2] Devi-McGleish, Y., Cox, DJ. (2018) *'From Wergild to a Way Forward? English Restorative Justice in its Historical Context'*, Wolverhampton Law Journal, 1 (1), pp 21-40.

[3] *Journals of tours through Wales,* NLW MS 18256C. The second source for Parker's comments is *Miscellaneous tours and descriptive memoranda of John Parker,* NLW MS 19382E, which includes *The Gothic tour in Carnarvonshire* in 1828 and the *Welch Tour* of 1829 as well as notes and memoranda on Gothic architecture and the screens at Llanrwst and Conwy.

All the Parker quotations included in the text are taken from these manuscript sources.

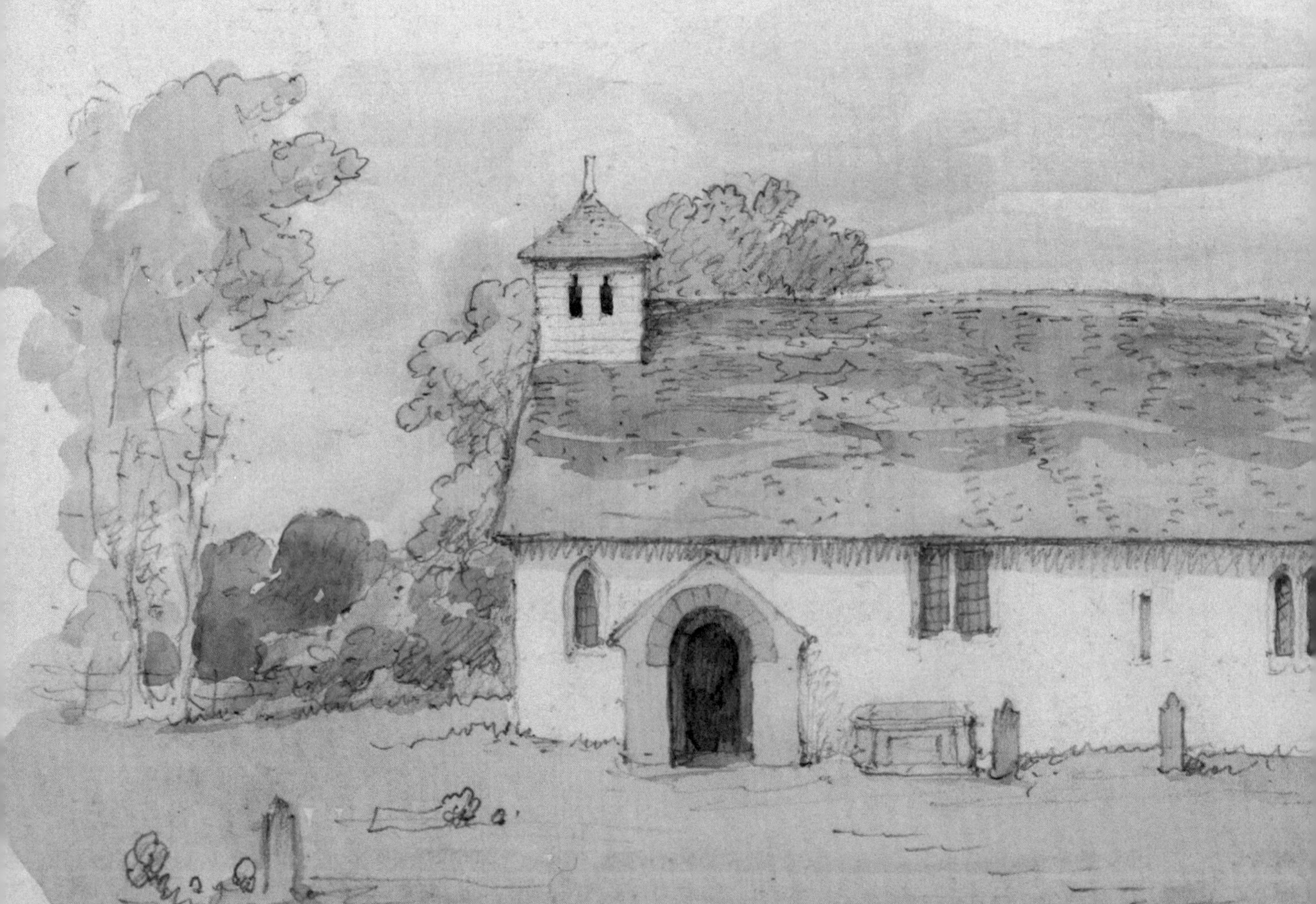

Chapter Two
Parker, the Anglican clergyman

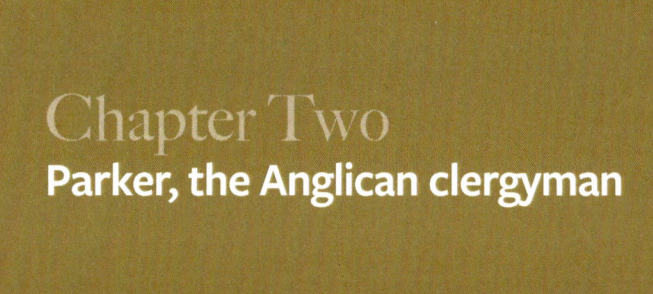

'Llanmarewic Church 1827'

Parker was content to spend his life as the incumbent of small country parishes; his duties were not onerous and he enjoyed the freedom which a private income afforded him to travel extensively. He owed his first two ecclesiastical appointments to Bishop Luxmoore. While he was staying at Bodowen, near Barmouth, with his uncle, he received a letter from the bishop on 24 June 1823 'offering me the curacy of Moreton Chapel'. Moreton (or Morton) was a chapel of the parish church in Oswestry and Parker's appointment probably also owed something to the influence of his father as Sweeney Hall is less than a mile to the north. (The present church replaced the chapel Parker knew, being built in 1873 to serve the new parish of Morton, which was created from the parishes of Oswestry and Llanyblodwel.) Parker stayed at Morton until 1827 and then moved to Llanmyrewig near Newtown until 1844, when he became vicar of Llanyblodwel, just on the English side of the border, six miles south-west of Sweeney Hall, where he stayed until his death in 1860.

Moreton Chapel 1790, Edward Williams, by permission of Shropshire Archives

Only once, in 1832, does he voice his frustration at his lowly position and lack of influence in the church. He recorded an hour's conversation at the palace in St Asaph on 11 September with Bishop Carey, Luxmoore's successor, about his request for the assistance of a curate. The bishop 'threw objections in the way of all that I proposed without expressing the slightest intention of helping me out of my present situation'. Parker added that 'I have sacrificed much for the Church already and if it had been in my power would sacrifice yet more.' At the palace he saw a portrait of the late Bishop Luxmoore, which prompted him to suppose that 'had he lived, [he] might have done something for me but his giving me my present living was a gift that I would rather not have accepted'. (In which case why did he stay at Llanmyrewig for a further 12 years?) He ended his account of this disappointing visit to St Asaph with another disillusioned comment on his predicament. 'Alas! how difficult it is to obtain even a moderate income in the church of England! how lowering and vexatious are the embarrassments that surround us! I call my living a popish living, for it forbids me to marry, and if I had not other means it would almost command me [to] abstain from meat!'

Here, Parker is uncharacteristically wallowing in self-pity and it must have tried the patience of his superior. He was appointed to Llanmyrewig, the second smallest parish in Montgomeryshire (Snead being the smallest) with a population of about 200, as a well-educated young man with a considerable private income. From 1845 to 1854, he received an allowance of £100 a quarter from his parents, later increased to nearly £500; no figures survive for the earlier years but it is likely he always had a substantial private income. (When his father died in 1848, John inherited the Sweeney estate and three properties in Leicester Square, London, as

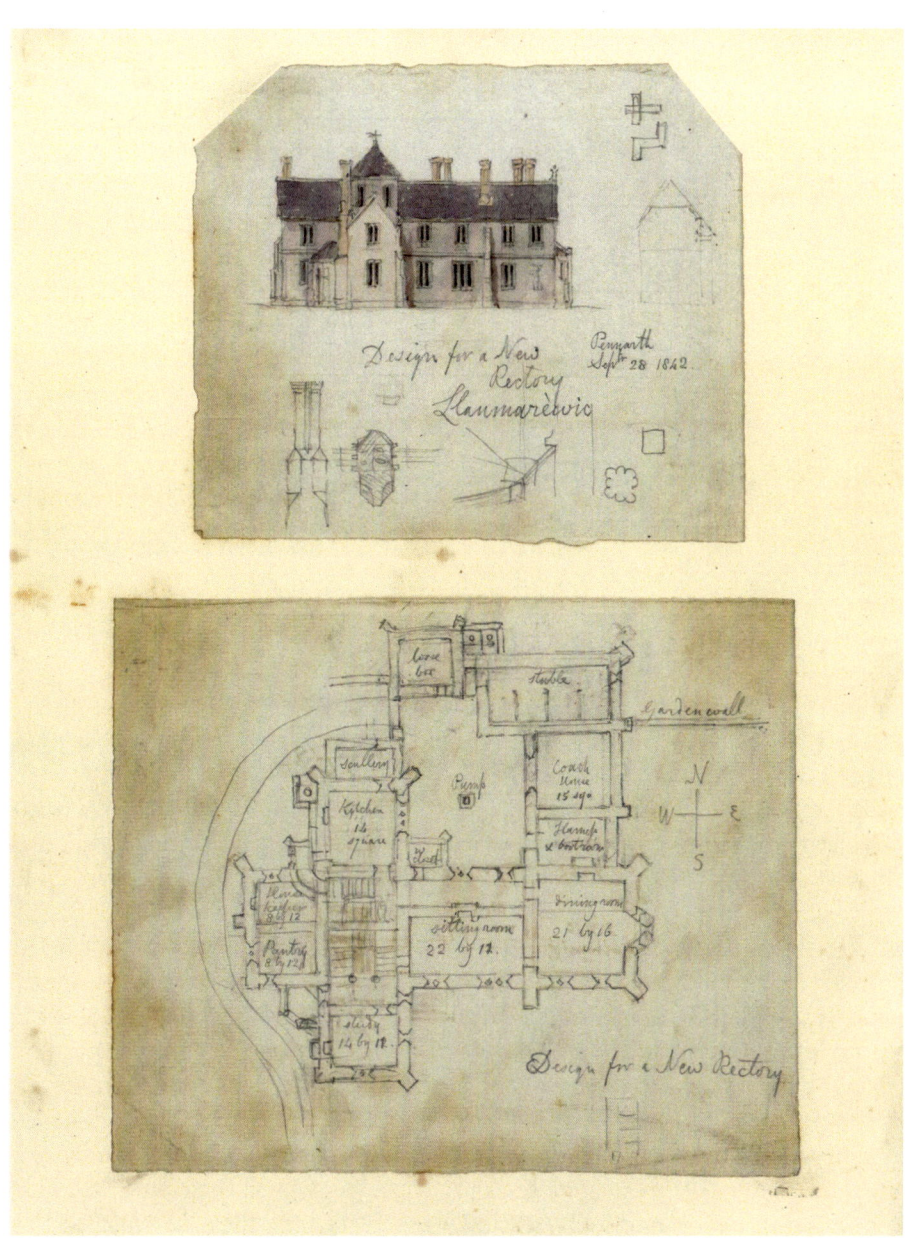

'Design for a New Rectory Llanmarewic'

Penarth, Parker's home when he was Rector of Llanmyrewig

well as houses in Lower Brook Street, Oswestry.)[4] As rector of Llanmyrewig, he lived at Penarth, a substantial farmhouse more than adequate for a bachelor. Among his sketches are the plan and elevation for a new rectory at Llanmyrewig, which show a large house designed around a courtyard with stabling for four horses, a coach house, harness and boot rooms. This was never built but it shows the scale of accommodation he considered suitable for a country clergyman. He also spent considerable sums on the rebuilding of Llanmyrewig church. So much for the 'popish living' he complained of after his fruitless interview with the bishop in 1832.

In fact, a curate left the year Parker arrived and for six years he had no assistance; it was towards the end of this period that he had his confrontation with the bishop. In the following year, he was granted his wish and from then until he moved to Llanyblodwel he had two curates in succession, the second of whom replaced him as rector in 1844. But one wonders what Bishop Carey thought about the importunate priest who spent so many summer days on the roads to Capel Curig, Barmouth and much further afield.

As an Anglican clergyman, Parker was one of the largest group of tourists who visited Wales and whose writings helped to make the area well known. These clerical tourists' visits to Wales involved frequent – and in some cases – lengthy absences from their parishes, which were left in the care of curates. Parker was one of a growing number of clerics from gentry families who were appointed to Montgomeryshire benefices in the first part of the nineteenth-century. Such men often played a prominent part in local affairs beyond their ecclesiastical duties, serving as magistrates and Poor Law Guardians. They lived in commodious rectories, many of which were rebuilt at this time. Parker was a conscientious incumbent compared with some of his clerical neighbours; in nearby Newtown, George Foxton, rector from 1815 until his death in 1844, spent most of his life in Gloucestershire, while the local squire of Newtown Hall, the Reverend George Arthur Evors, was the absentee rector of Rudbaxton in Pembrokeshire from 1806 until 1844.

When he moved to Llanyblodwel, Parker succeeded James Donne, who had been vicar since 1798, a living he occupied while also serving as the headmaster of Oswestry School until 1833. Llanyblodwel was in the care of curates until Donne retired there from the headmastership. For the last sixteen years of his life at Llanyblodwel, Parker travelled less frequently and spent much of his time on his building projects; as vicar he was assisted by a succession of five curates.

While some of the clergy attracted criticism for their pluralism and non-residence, men like Parker, although not devoting all their time to parochial affairs, were respected for their learning and, in his case, for his generosity. Parker was typical of the many Victorian clergymen who made significant contributions to literature, philosophy, history and archaeology. The learned journals of national and local societies reveal just how many of their contributors and supporters were clerics. The Cambrian Archaeological Association, of which Parker was an enthusiastic member, was founded in 1846 in response to an appeal by ninety 'antiquaries', thirty-six of whom were clergymen. The drawings that he made of screens and fonts, although not published, were 'put at the disposal of our Association; and not a few of them will be remembered by those members who partook of his hospitality at the Welshpool meeting' held in August 1856.

His travels gave him opportunities to experience the religious practices of non-Anglican denominations and these he reported vividly and at some length in his journals. The comments he made on his European tour in 1827 are a reminder of the visceral hostility to Catholicism which persisted in Britain in the nineteenth-century. In June 1827, while staying at Ostend (appropriately for an Englishman at the judiciously named Waterloo Hotel), he stepped into a Catholic church. Here he saw 'old men and women were praying to the statues and pictures there, especially to a hideous figure of the Virgin Mary … the dress of this idol was of gold tissue with a lace veil and silver crown, her face was painted like a doll's … I stood for a long time observing them and felt convinced that their worship in the sight of God was as completely idolatrous as that of the ancient heathens. In fact it was dreadful to be an actual witness of Christianity so corrupted.' His appreciation of church architecture in the Netherlands was coloured by the furnishings he found inside. Antwerp's Notre Dame tower 'is a magnificent object', but a statue of the crucifixion 'I think … was the most offensive & absurd exhibition of popish art that we have yet seen'.

Journeys into Snowdonia took Parker to the heartlands of Welsh nonconformity. The results of the only religious census taken in Britain, in 1851, gave the Established Church an awful shock.[5] The statistics showed that in Wales Anglicans were greatly outnumbered by Nonconformists; chapels offered more than twice as many 'sittings' than the churches and of the attendances on Sunday 30 March, four-fifths were in chapels. Whether the preponderance of Dissent was as great as some commentators claimed, it was clear that the state church, with its privileged position and supported by tithes paid by all landlords or tenants, no longer retained the loyalty of the Welsh people. Any visitor to Wales in the first half of the nineteenth-century would have noted the proliferation of chapels and drawn the obvious conclusion about popular religious practice. The Anglican church had recognised the threat from Nonconformity a generation before the 1851 census and churches were being restored – often this amounted to rebuilding – and some new churches were commissioned. Parker played a part in the Anglican fightback in the rebuilding work he did at his two parish churches. But in Wales in particular, the Anglicans' response was too little, too late and, while they had made up some lost ground, by the end of the century Nonconformity remained the religion of the large majority.

Parker was more sympathetic to the Nonconformist services he attended than those he saw in Catholic churches in the Netherlands, but his antipathy towards the architecture of chapels deeply influenced his views. Parker's devotion to Gothic architecture was based on his belief that it was the only style appropriate for a place of worship. 'No style of architecture has displayed so practical and solemn a character as the gothic … Therefore no other style should be employed for

Revd John Parker of Sweeney, Vicar of Llanyblodwell.
c. 1850 oil on board, Margaret Giles (1803-1887)

churches … Gothic is the development of Christianity in art.' He was concerned that the style of the rapidly spreading chapels was affecting church building: 'The internal aspect of the Meeting House I greatly fear is beginning to react upon the church, and we shall see reproduced, the same barren squareness and flatness, and whiteness which hitherto have been peculiar to the uncatholic dissenters.'

In Caernarfon in 1830, he saw 'two conspicuous meeting houses, one vulgar gothic Wesleyan chapel, the other Calvinistic, Whitfield's followers.' At Tal-y-bont, 'I saw nothing worthy of notice but the pompous vulgarities of two rival meeting houses within a few yards of each other. These hideous buildings everywhere unsightly, give to many a Welsh landscape a character of naked ugliness.'[6] In an outburst about the destruction of the screen at Llangurig, he referred to the Dissenters and 'their own vile meeting houses'. It is worth noting that few of the chapels Parker saw have survived; such was the success of Nonconformity that the buildings were enlarged, sometimes more than once. Towards the end of the century, Nonconformists adopted versions of the Gothic style, not that this would have appeased Parker.

While he was no friend of Dissenters, he was interested in their beliefs and practices. On a Sunday in 1832, he walked to Llanberis church with 'my former guide up Snowdon' and they discussed the differences between the Anglicans and the Calvinistic Methodists. 'He could not understand that authority was distinct from personal character, but at length, when the cases of Balaam, Caiaphas and Judas were mentioned he acknowledged it in them.' On his way back from church, Parker stopped at a cottage door 'where a dissenting minister of the Independent persuasion was addressing a small congregation. He was a middle aged, rather good looking man, a schoolmaster whose residence was a few miles off and his manner was, in general, pleasing. His voice was also good … He used much action. Sometimes one, sometimes both hands, not however affectedly, but only when it seemed natural to him. His hearers were continually repeating amen, as a sign of approbation at the end of any sentence that pleased them.'

After dinner at the inn, Parker, again with his guide, strolled down to the Calvinistic Methodist chapel nearby and 'when I saw the congregation collecting I went into the chapel myself'. The first part of the service impressed Parker; a psalm was 'well sung, with the congregation joining in' and then the minister began preaching: 'there was no false doctrine, but a slowness and dryness of expression and manner, strongly contrasted with what followed.' (It seems that the minister recognised Parker and for his benefit he spoke at first in English, 'making excuses for his awkwardness'.) Later, the minister reverted to Welsh and, 'although temperate at first, by degrees the tones of his voice became wilder … the preacher now became still more violent, he stamped with his feet, flung his arms about and raved. Then some women began to cry aloud in reply and at last his voice was drowned in their outcries. He continued for a wonderful length of time roaring and raving while they rivalled him, as being several against one.' By the end of the service 'I observed two women who were in a state of convulsion near the pulpit; these two had been most violent in their ejaculations.'

The effects of the service persisted late into the night; loud cries could be heard at the chapel, which prompted Parker to go outside at ten o'clock when he 'witnessed a scene of horror that I shall never forget. There were four boys and about six girls about 15 or 16 years old, the boys younger, all raving mad!! their friends looking on, while these unhappy wretches unconscious of all around them did nothing but ejaculate without intermission, lifting up their arms and rolling over the pews and benches.' He heard such cries until nearly midnight. This experience confirmed for Parker all his worst fears of the fanaticism of some branches of nonconformity. He compared the effects of this service to 'a well-known specimen of Romish fraud – the liquefaction of the blood of St Januarius. The madness of superstition exhibits the same features in almost all ages countries and nations.' Parker feared for the physical and mental health of the young people thus aroused to a state of frenzy. He was also anxious for his church, wondering 'can such men as these fanatics overthrow an apostolic establishment?'[7]

Wherever he was on a Sunday, Parker attended the nearest Anglican church and he was usually complimentary about the performance of his fellow clerics. On 30 June 1833, he went to Bangor cathedral for the English service, which followed the Welsh one. Mr Cotton, the vicar choral, took the service and Parker was impressed by 'his good voice and ... earnest manner ... he preached a very good sermon dwelling much on the duty of praying for the king, the anniversary of William the 4th's accession occurred on Wednesday last.' He sometimes attended Welsh services. On his first recorded tour in September 1819, he went to Llanberis church: 'thin congregation ... The Welch service is very pleasing to hear. Richer sounds, slower pronunciation than in English.' (That service was at St Peris church in Nant Peris, the original village – the present church in Llanberis dates from the 1880s.) In July 1832, he went again to Llanberis, where 'Mr Williams Junior read the service and preached in Welch.' Here Parker was 'vexed at seeing the clergyman's hat put on the communion table, and others also belonging to the congregation'. (He might have been at a seventeenth-century Anglican service where Puritans did likewise.) On Sunday 30 August 1846, he 'attended Welsh morning service at Towyn Church at 11 and evening service in English at 3 o'clock'.

He was aware of the strain that providing bilingual services put on the local clergy. At Aberystwyth in May 1840, he went to the morning service 'at the new chapel of ease' where, to his dismay, the pulpit and reading desk 'are in front of the chancel', which meant that the view towards the altar was obscured. On Sunday, three clergymen had 'seven duties to divide among them', with four services – two in Welsh – at the new chapel, two at Llanbadarn and one at the National School. Parker 'trembled for his [Mr Hughes, the vicar of Llanbadarn] failing strength'. He then added a personal note: 'the strength of a clergyman fails first in the prayers; in the responses or the sermon the continuous nature of the subject in some degree sustains him, but I always feel that there is something more trying and overpowering in the comprehensive petitions of our prayerbook than in any other part of a clergyman's duty. I never attend the performance of divine service by others without some degree of thankfulness that I am excused on those occasions.'

[4] Will of T.N. Parker, National Archives PROB 11/2087/11.

[5] For an introduction to religion in Victorian Wales see *The Welsh Church, from Reformation to Disestablishment, 1603–1920*, Glanmor Williams, William Jacob, Nigel Yates, Frances Knight, 2007, Part 111:1780–1850.

[6] NLW MS 19382E, number 8 on Gothic Art.

[7] 'Jumpers' was the term used to describe people gripped by such frenzied enthusiasm; for similar reports by other observers, see Michael Freeman, op. cit.

Intended for the "Rayengers" but considered as a failure in the etching by John Ruskin. J.R.

Chapter Three
The Passengers

'Maen Du, Intended for The Passengers but considered as a failure in the etching.'

Many of the visitors who toured Wales during Parker's lifetime published accounts of their experiences based on their journals, diaries or letters; in some cases, they included sketches of the most spectacular sights. Parker's only venture into this overcrowded field is *The Passengers: containing the Celtic Annals*[8], published in 1831. The book illustrates his three great enthusiasms: the scenery of North Wales, Gothic art and his love of poetry. It is in two parts: the first, in the form of a 'Dialogue between Three Gentlemen', recounts a journey to the summit of Snowdon and the second is a long poem 'incidental to the subject [and] as a specimen of Greek versification in the English language. The whole adapted for aiding the Tourist in North Wales.'

The beautifully drawn frontispiece introduces Parker's architectural obsession, the search for the perfect example of Gothic architecture. It shows the porch of a church decorated with intricate tracery, pinnacles and crockets and beyond the entrance an equally elaborate screen which leads into the church. The author explained that the drawing was based 'in general design on Tongres cathedral in the Netherlands', while the tracery derived from 'an elegant ruin at Bararach on the Rhine' modified by 'the foliations in the panelled roof of Crosby Hall, London'.[9] The choice of buildings from the Netherlands, the Rhineland and England illustrates Parker's wide architectural interests and knowledge.

The journey starts in Oswestry, where so many of Parker's explorations of Snowdonia began. 'On a fine summer morning, in the latter end of July 182*, three outside Passengers left Oswestry by one of the morning coaches for Capel Cerig [*sic*], about half-past seven o'clock upon a tour through North Wales.' There follows what to modern taste is a very contrived account in the form of a conversation between the passengers. In an attempt to introduce some realism into the opening scene, Parker has the coachman and the guard chatting about the passengers listed on 'the way-bill'. The coachman gives the names as Larndon, Allansley and Clanvoy and adds 'Clanvoy; that's he as comes up this way twice or thrice every summer.' Clanvoy is Parker, who takes the lead in the conversations that make up the book; it was true that by 1831 he was already a regular passenger on this, his favourite journey to the heart of Snowdonia. Note that the three gentlemen, who could have afforded the comfort of seats inside the coach, travelled 'outside'; Parker wanted his friends to see the countryside and to point out places of interest. The journey is an opportunity for Clanvoy to act as a tour guide in response to a series of questions obligingly put by the other two. They pass Chirk castle, where, according to their guide, 'Harrison of Chester has lately done some good Gothic vaulting.' To which Allansley responds, on cue, 'What? The architect of that beautiful Doric Entrance in Chester castle?' Which prompts Clanvoy to inform his companion that it is the same man 'who, I dare say ... repents of what he did there. An ancient English fortress ought not to give way even to the Parthenon itself.' After this magisterial rebuke, the third traveller can only ask, 'Are we still in Shropshire?'

This didactic style continues, with Clanvoy taking every opportunity to tell his friends about the history of the area and expound on the glories of the countryside they are passing through. While the coach stops to change horses at Llangollen and, after some conversation about the Ladies of Plas Newydd, Allansley abruptly changes the subject and asks, 'What sort of churches are there in North Wales? Are they in general worth notice?' Clanvoy seizes his chance and launches into a lengthy answer, which includes references to St

*'The north porch of Tongres cathedral,
Wed June 18 1827'*

Winifred's Well, Milan cathedral, the Reformation, Palladio and the Dean of Christ Church. But what Parker emphasises in this response is a subject to which he returned frequently in his journals – the misleading impression given by many Welsh churches which belied the treasures inside. 'In general they look like the chief barn of the neighbourhood.' But in these unprepossessing buildings you may find 'wood-carving so exquisite and original, that, if it were placed in some English cathedral, the lover of Gothic would be in raptures of admiration'. Wooden chancel screens with their galleries were to be the subject of some of Parker's most beautiful and meticulous drawings.

But for the companions of 1831, the objective was the summit of Snowdon, rather than the study of church furnishings. Here again their leader was the expert. When they reached the inn at Capel Curig, Clanvoy asked for Evan Jones, a guide he 'would recommend ... to any friends of mine, as an intelligent, experienced attendant for a party to take with them up Snowdon'. (Evan Jones appears on lists of Snowdon guides as active between 1803 and 1828.) However, Jones had been 'pre-engaged by a "gentleman from London" who is going to see Dolwyddelan under the impression that it is a kind of Windsor castle ... and Evan Jones ... does nothing to undeceive him.' (One suspects that Parker's sympathy was with the guide rather than the naive tourist.) The absence of Evan Jones is not a problem; Clanvoy assures his friends that 'I know the mountain better than any guide, I have been up there alone, or in company in all kinds of weather ... do not, therefore be afraid of my leading you astray.' Such self-confidence was justified given the number of times Parker had by 1831 climbed Snowdon and its adjoining peaks. The three ascended the mountain the next day, and their guide and teacher identified peaks and lakes as well as lecturing them on the botanical specimens which are unique to Snowdon. The views from the summit more than satisfied the expectations of gentlemen reared on the Romantic poets and the theories of the picturesque. Allansley 'cried out with rapture ... I never saw an effect altogether so sublime and ghastly!' Their appreciation of the magnificence of the mountain was dimmed only by the actual summit, which was marked, to Larndon's annoyance, 'by this heap of stonework, and those planks above it, that prevent our turning round in the same place to see the whole panorama'. Clanvoy explains that this structure had been erected because so many visitors were 'carrying off the identical highest piece of the rock that was to be found'.

Apart from the frontispiece, Parker included only one drawing in The Passengers, a panoramic view of Snowdon and Capel Curig. He proposed adding a sketch of Maen Du, the great boulder also known as the 'Poetmaking stone', but it was 'considered as a failure in the etching'; this was a subject he would revisit many times.[10] While The Passengers is an idealised account of the numerous journeys he made to Snowdonia, Parker's journals provide a record of the real conditions under which his travels were undertaken.

'Snowden and Capel-Cerig from a Hill above the Irish Road...Morning'

[8] The book can be read online.
[9] Crosby Hall was built in 1466 and originally stood on Bishopsgate in the city, but was moved to Cheyne Walk, Chelsea in 1910.
[10] The annotated drawing is at the start of this chapter.

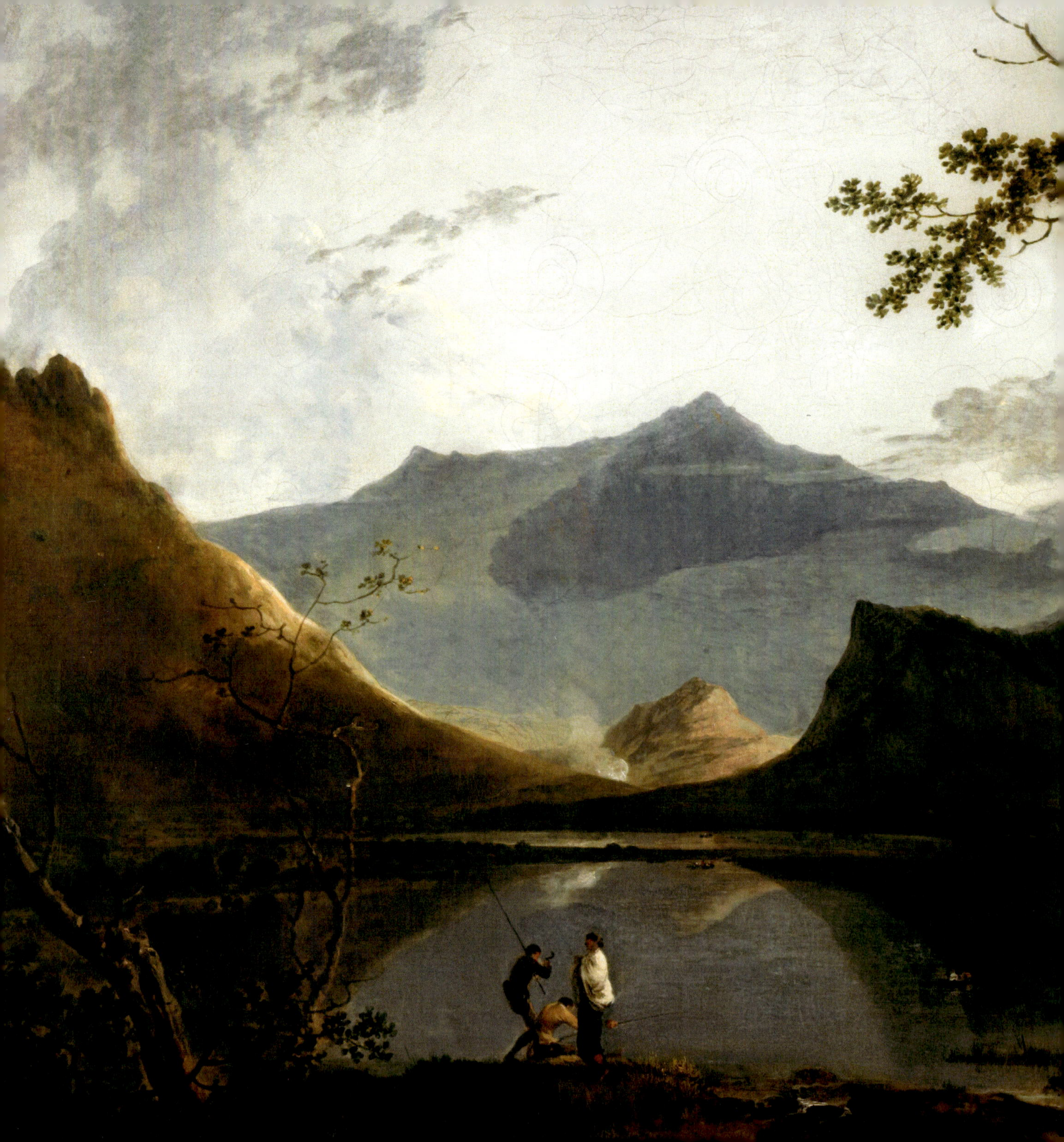

Chapter Four
The Picturesque and the 'discovery' of North Wales

Richard Wilson (1714-82), *Snowdon from Llyn Nantlle*,
Walker Art Gallery, Liverpool

In the medieval and early modern period, the land was something to be worked, while mountains and forests were dangerous places to be avoided if possible; by the eighteenth-century attitudes towards the landscape altered radically. 'In the first decades of the eighteenth-century virtually no artist would bother going to North Wales, the Lake District or the Highlands of Scotland. Towards the end they barely went anywhere else.'[11] The reasons for this revolutionary change are numerous and varied: increasing prosperity gave more people the means and the leisure to indulge a taste for travel, which was made easier by improvements to turnpike roads and more comfortable vehicles.

Visitors to Wales, like travellers to the Lake District and Scotland, were also influenced by the Romantic movement, which fostered an enthusiasm for rugged landscapes and led to the pursuit of what were termed the Picturesque and the Sublime. While much of rural England and Wales was being tamed by the enclosure of common land and the open fields, Romantics sought the mountains for inspiration. When the continent was convulsed by the French Revolution and later by the Napoleonic wars – both of which made travel to Europe difficult, if not dangerous – the wilder parts of Britain saw a great increase in the number of visitors. The Highlands, the Lakes and Snowdonia proved popular substitutes for the Alps.

If one man can claim the credit for the change in attitude towards the wilder parts of Britain it was William Gilpin, 'a retiring clergyman-schoolmaster from Surrey' who wrote up accounts of his summer holidays, most famously his *Observations on the River Wye*.[12] This illustrated account of a journey he made in 1770 was published in 1782 and became a bestseller, prompting travellers to take to the roads, rivers and lakes to record their experiences of what they saw in diaries, journals

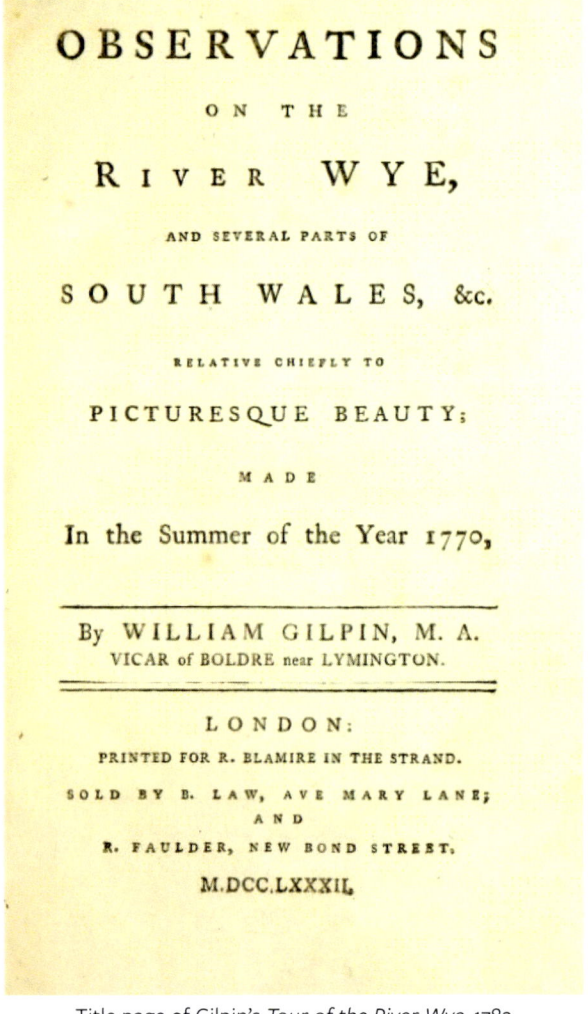

Title page of Gilpin's *Tour of the River Wye*, 1782

and sketches. Gilpin's work is both more and less than a travel guide; he provides little historical or anecdotal information to entertain the reader, being more concerned to educate the traveller in how to appreciate the countryside. He was the best-known advocate of the

A page from Pennant's *Tour in Wales*, 1784

Picturesque, a set of ideas which influenced philosophers, artists, writers and landscape gardeners, including Edmund Burke, Wordsworth, Gainsborough, Turner, Repton and Richard Payne Knight. Henceforth the countryside was to be appreciated as an inspiration for sensations which elevated the mind and the soul. There was much debate about the composition of a true picturesque scene: nature was sometimes deficient and needed improving but undoubtedly mountains, rivers, lakes and waterfalls were required subjects; grazing cows and sheep and one or two small figures complemented the landscape.

From 1780, following Gilpin, scores of books were published describing the beauties and significant landmarks of the new tourist destinations. Michael Freeman has identified over 1,200 accounts of tours in Wales between 1700 and 1900, of which 326 were published.[13] Many travellers did not stray from the routes and sites recommended by guidebooks, which became increasingly formulaic. Their predictability was noticed in 1832: 'a foreigner collating our books of Welsh travel, to plan his course "in search of the picturesque," would find such a uniformity in the direction to a few places (so hackneyed as to have become like household words), to the exclusion of all Wales besides, that he would consider the Principality as a wilderness, a waste in point of interest, containing some scattered oases of singular beauty, which have been the only resting-places for the tasteful tourist ... [and] ... these it has been the aim of our travellers to forget to visit."[14] Parker refers scathingly to one guidebook in 1820 when staying in Caernarfon at The Goat inn, he found a small book 'calling itself "Letters from Snowdon" which comprised a greater number of falsehoods and inconsistencies, than I could have expected to find in so small a publication'.

Today the best known account of Wales written in the later eighteenth-century is Thomas Pennant's *Tour in Wales*, published in two volumes in 1778 and 1781, based on three journeys he made between 1773 and 1776.[15] Though Pennant wrote some fifty years earlier than Parker, a comparison of the two men's work is revealing. Both were gentlemen of means who lived near the border between Wales and England. They shared a keen interest in the history of Wales, and both visited and described many of the same buildings and were enthusiastic in their appreciation of the mountains of Snowdonia. Pennant's account of his ascent of Snowdon is 'a classic of its kind, written in exact descriptive prose mercifully economical with the rhetorical flourishes that bedevil most of his contemporaries.'[16] A similar compliment can be paid to Parker but his accounts of climbing Snowdon are scattered in his journals and not edited for publication like Pennant's.

In Pennant's work there is a great deal of information about the industry and economy of the areas he visited, whereas Parker takes little interest in either; he barely mentions the rapidly expanding slate industry which was reshaping the landscape and society. The occupations of the inhabitants, other than those involved in travel and hospitality, are rarely referred to. He visited Beddgelert many times but, unlike most visitors, he made no reference to the story of Gelert and Prince Llywelyn which gave the village its name. For Pennant, the ancestry of the gentry families was of considerable importance; Parker visited their houses and inspected their monuments but was less attracted to genealogy. In this respect, and because he included a lot more historical information, Pennant's work is similar to the county histories which were published at the time, such as Theophilus Jones's *A History of the County of Brecknock*. Pennant's written style seems to the modern reader rather archaic but Parker's has a freshness and immediacy. Whereas Pennant had Moses Griffith to provide the illustrations, Parker was his own artist and his sketches and paintings stand comparison with those by Griffith. Lastly, and the biggest difference, is that one author was published in expensive, illustrated editions for his subscribers, while Parker's work rests, rarely read, in the vaults of the National Library of Wales.

Pennant's volumes were not handy pocket-books for the traveller or tourist but that gap was filled by the Reverend Richard Warner's two *Walks through Wales* published in 1799 and 1800. Richard Warner had been one of Gilpin's curates and clearly he was influenced by his mentor's passion for walking and the countryside. Warner's two *Walks*, which combined historical information with anecdotes written in a conversational style, attracted a wide readership. Although their books were different in style and content, Warner was keen to pay tribute to Pennant, and was invited to Downing, Pennant's house near Holywell, to meet 'the "literary veteran" by whom the public has been so much amused and so much instructed'.[17]

Among Warner's enthusiastic readers was John Britton, whose twenty-seven volumes of *The Beauties of England and Wales*, published from 1801 onwards, did much to stimulate interest in the country's historic buildings.[18] In his autobiography, Britton recalled that 'I read it [Walks Through Wales] with avidity ... and found that such writing did not require much recondite learning, and need not be encumbered by dull details of genealogy, manorial and parochial history, and useless lists of rectors and vicars ... [it was] calculated to excite curiosity in the reader.'[19] With Britton, this succession of topographical writers reaches Parker, who was described in his obituary as 'an intimate and friend of earnest-minded Britton'. Had he been a published author, Parker, with his facility as a writer and artist, would have surely earned an honoured place among these figures.

Such was the literary and intellectual context for Parker's journeys. The Picturesque was one of the subjects discussed by the three travellers in The Passengers and it is clear that Parker was well acquainted with the concept. When Clanvoy lauded the beauty of Llyn Tegid (Bala lake), which he considered 'much undervalued', he stated that 'the lake is about four miles in length, almost as long as any picturesque lake need be.' Another component was 'a grazing farm [which] will also be the most picturesque; for cattle require shelter, and groves, into which they may go during the heat of the day.' As the coach approached Snowdon, Clanvoy pointed to the way in which the summit hid behind 'rocky banks' and said, 'I do think this mysterious veiling of Snowdon, as you proceed into it, until the time when it comes forth in full grandeur, is one of the most alluring specimens of the picturesque I know.'

Years later, in 1846, after a tour of Merionethshire and north Montgomeryshire, Parker summed up his thoughts: 'During this tour of twelve days I have added something to my experience of the picturesque. I have seen great abundance of rich materials, but those materials were seldom arranged so as to have their full effect. In the neighbourhood of Dolgelly the torrent scenery, smothered in copse wood is more an object of sound than of sight. Hundreds of small oaks must be felled before those wild cascades and their gigantic rocks can meet the eye of the tourist or the artist. In some spots the gorse and heath, in blossom together, add greatly to the colouring of the landscape. Yet of heath, I observe, that it is apt sometimes rather to diminish than to add [to] the effect of rocks, And therefore I will deal cautiously with it in my landscape gardening at Blodwel.'

He was, however, a man of independent judgement and although influenced by current ideas about the Picturesque – and later the Sublime – he was no slave to modish fashion. He described with pen and brush what he considered worth recording whether it was on the tourists' recommended list of 'stations' from which picturesque views were to be admired or not.

---

[11] Susan Owens, *Spirit of Place: Artists, Writers & the British Landscape* Thames and Hudson, 2020, 139. The book covers the subject from the earliest times to the present with particular emphasis on the eighteenth and nineteenth centuries and the evolution of the Picturesque movement. Wales, however, receives less attention than it deserves – for example, there is no reference to Thomas Pennant.

[12] For Gilpin, see Owens, *op. cit.*, 152 et seq.

[13] Freeman, *op. cit.*

[14] Anon, 'Conversations of poets among the Mountains', in the *Cambrian Quarterly & Celtic Repository,* Vol. IV, No. 16 (October 1832), 433–455.

[15] For Pennant and other commentators see Rosemary Sweet, *Antiquaries: The Discovery of the past in Eighteenth-Century Britain* (Hambledon and London, 2004).

[16] Jim Perrin's *Snowdon: The Story of a Welsh Mountain* Gomer, 2012 is an entertaining and informative introduction to Snowdon, its history and myths, and the impact of man on this landscape. It is enlivened by acerbic footnotes.

[17] Warner, *A Second Walk Through Wales,* 4th edition (1813), 282.

[18] For Britton, see Rosemary Hill, *Time's Witness, History in the Age of Romanticisim* (Allen Lane, 2021), passim.

[19] Britton, *Autobiography* (1850), 168.

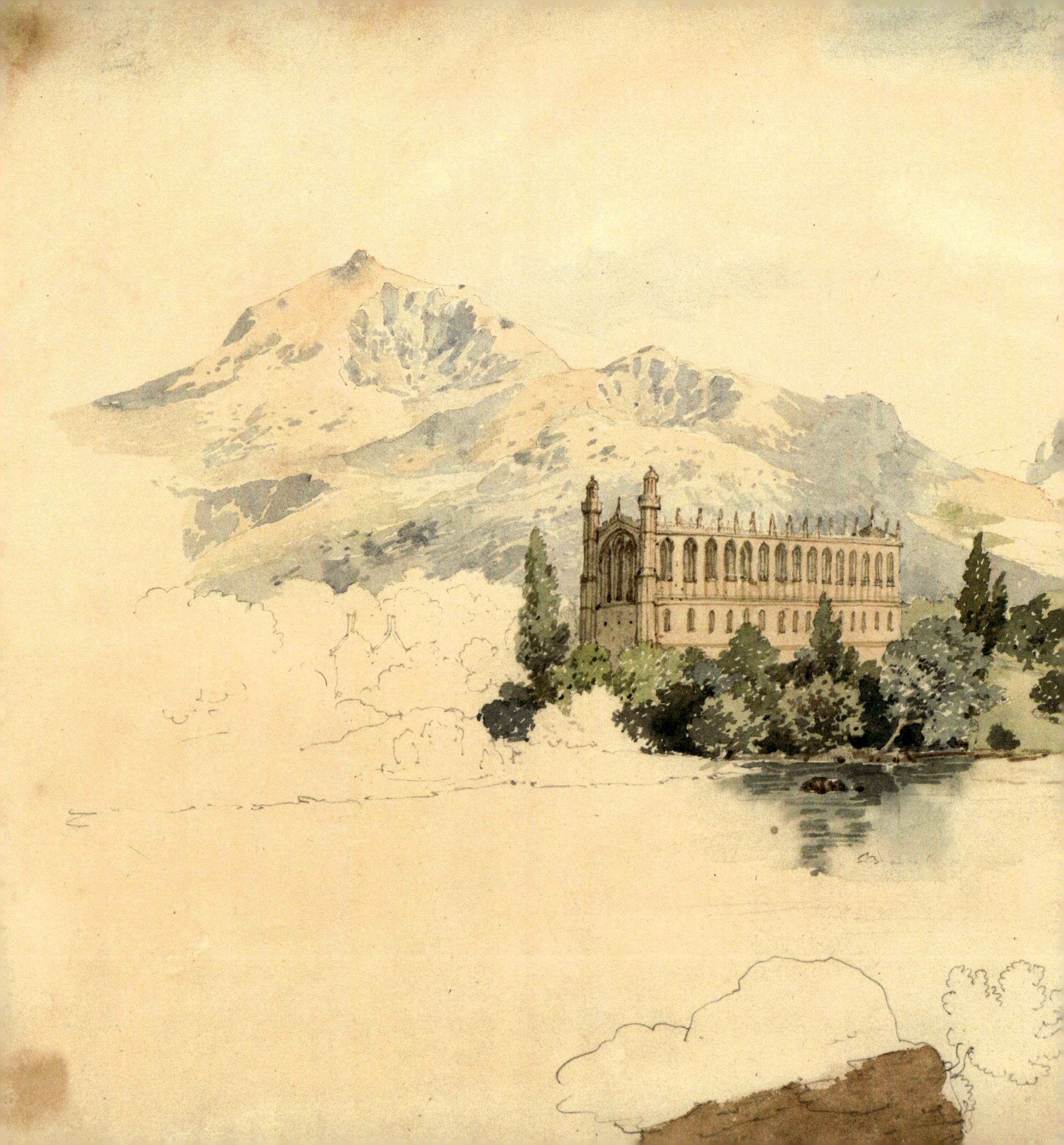

Chapter Five
Parker's journeys to North Wales

Eton College chapel and Snowdon

Parker's love affair – and the phrase in this case is no mere cliché – with Snowdonia began when he was an Eton schoolboy and persisted until his death. One of his earliest watercolours, dated 1812 when he was 14, shows an outline of the principal peaks of the area with Moel Siabod at the centre; his last drawing done in June 1860 is of Caernarfon castle, which he visited on his final journey; he died only two months later on August 31st. In August 1822, he climbed Moel Siabod and recalled the last time he was there: 'I was a schoolboy. On the eve of returning to Eton, I had snatched a hasty tour into Wales, and we found ourselves upon the brink of this precipice, at seven oclock in a fine evening. In returning back to Capel cerig [sic] we lost our way among the marshes and with difficulty regained the proper path. The fourth day from that beheld me at Eton, my imagination entirely full of mountain scenery, and the odious contrast of insipid plains and of noisy schoolfellows rendered me quite heartsick.' His painting of Eton chapel with Snowdon in the background graphically illustrates the schoolboy's yearning for the mountains.

When he travelled, it was as an explorer rather than a tourist, especially in Snowdonia. He visited the well-known sites, but often ventured off what tracks there were to investigate byways and hidden places. This was in part due to his natural curiosity, but also because he visited the same area many times and got to know parts of Snowdonia better than some of the inhabitants. In July 1832, he was pleased to be able to point out to his guide that to the south-west of the summit of Snowdon there were four – not two – lakes as his guide supposed; Parker wrote that he 'convinced [him] by ocular demonstration'. When he walked or rode among the mountains he noted not just the dramatic, picturesque views but the unusual flora of the region; he was no mean botanist and his drawings of wild flowers are among his most appealing works. He was fascinated by rocks and wrote eloquently about their size and shape and how they added drama to the landscape.

He had the advantage of visiting many gentry houses and parish churches before they were transformed by Victorian improvers and restorers. His drawings of screens and fonts are well known and some have been published, but there are many more which repay study. When he was not travelling, he indulged his love of architecture and was responsible for the dramatic, not to say melodramatic, transformation of his churches at Llanmyrewig and Llanyblodwel.

Parker travelled to much of the British Isles and to parts of western Europe and each expedition resulted in a journal and many sketches, though in some cases the writing ceases abruptly and we do not have a complete record. For this book – as an introduction to Parker – it is the visits to North Wales which are examined; because he went there so often they offer the most detailed and most heartfelt accounts of his attitudes and enthusiasms, as well as some of his best writing.

Snowdonia Panorama, 1812

June. 1820. Welch tour

The style of landscape prevailing in North Wales is of so peculiarly fine a cast that it is only after repeated visits that the full power of its beauty enters the mind; or that we can estimate the merits of those places which please indeed, or perhaps astonish at first, but which after a more intimate acquaintance, establish in us a permanent and heartfelt admiration.

I passed along the Irish road with my friend Neave, upon the eighteenth of June 1820, in a day which altogether displayed the mountains to great advantage, the calm and easy manner in which this road wind along regions of scattered rocks, and much precipice, gives to the mountains the advantage of contrast, and furnishes the traveller with a beautiful succession of picturesque situations.

On reaching Capel cerig, the tops of everything were all unclouded, but rather dim, about

A page from Parker's journal describing his Welch [sic] Tour beginning in June 1820, NLW MS 18256.

Between his first and last visits in 1810 and 1860, he made between 25 and 35 visits to different parts of North Wales, but they almost always included Snowdonia. The first visit which he recorded was in 1819, but he made sketches and paintings dated 1810–13 (when presumably he accompanied his parents on journeys) and also in 1817 and 1818. The dramatic picture of Llyn y Gader, on the front cover, dates from 1818. Between 1819 and 1824, he left detailed accounts of annual visits and again in 1826, 1828 and 1829. There is a painting of 'Pentre Voelas', dated 1825, which may represent another visit. He made brief excursions in 1828 and 1829 to Llanrwst and to the Llŷn Peninsula and there is a painting of 'Clynnog Vawr' dated 1830, which was probably completed after his visit there the previous year. He went three times in 1832, although one was an official visit to the bishop at St Asaph, but he took time to look at interesting churches and houses on his way. His longest stay in Snowdonia was for two weeks in 1833 at Capel Curig and Bangor. Between 1829 and 1833, he spent at least seven weeks in Snowdonia; he therefore got to know particular parts of the region, especially the environs of Capel Curig and Llanberis, better than many contemporary visitors.

There is a gap until the next journal, dated 1840. However, two drawings of 1834 place him on the 'Irish Road' (the present A5), from where he drew the mountain [Pen yr] Ole Wen, and a month later he sketched Cnicht. A solitary drawing of Tal-y-llyn (near Llanrwst) dates from 1841. He made two visits in the summer of 1846 and another the following year; these are the last recorded in a travel journal. However, he drew views of Llandudno in 1848 and the church at Conwy in 1849; in 1851 he was at Derwen Cross and Rug. These journeys do not include visits he made to places within a day's drive or ride of Sweeney or Llanyblodwel, including Valle Crucis, Pennant Melangell and Pistyll Rhaeadr.

John Parker's lifetime coincided with a transport revolution in Britain; turnpike trusts improved the roads, canals spread rapidly and in the 1830s the railways arrived.[20] All three resulted in significant changes not only to industry, commerce and society but also to the landscape. For Parker, the improvement in travel by road was the most important as it was not until the 1850s that he took journeys by rail. Turnpikes were toll roads controlled by trustees who looked to make a profit by charging travellers and then reinvesting some of that money improving the road and so attracting more traffic. Tolls varied according to how much wear and tear the vehicle (or animals) would cause to the road. Toll gates, usually with small houses attached, were built across the road at regular intervals and boards displayed the charges. Milestones and direction posts were set up.

By modern standards travel was still slow and, on his early tours,

Turnpike trust milestone near Newtown

Tollhouse at Llanfairpwll, Anglesey

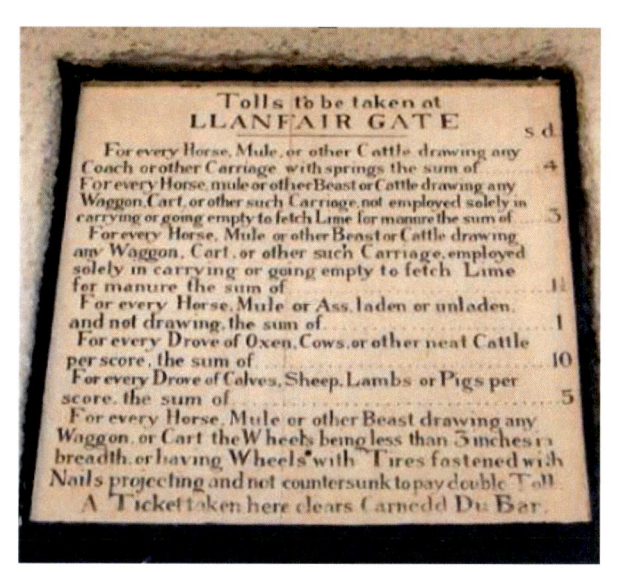

Tollhouse board of charges for use of the turnpike

Parker had to allow most of a day for the journey by coach from Oswestry to Capel Curig, but with improved roads and the increasing speed of coaches, he was able to cover surprising distances. Although he was the rector of Llanmyrewig until 1844, almost all his visits to Snowdonia started from his parents' home, Sweeney Hall, which was close to Oswestry, where he caught one of the coaches which ran along Telford's much improved 'Irish Road'. In 1828, on his return from a visit to Llanrwst and Conwy, he voiced his one complaint about the journeys from Llanmyrewig to North Wales: 'Left Pentre Voelas at 11 – after getting up at 5 to go on the Mail, which was full; dinner at Llangollen, Oswestry soon after 4 more food at Sweeney then back to Penarth, arrived at half past eleven heartily tired of the 25 miles between me and Sweeney.'

Since the Act of Union with Ireland in 1801, the government had made speedy communication between London and Dublin a high priority, hence the great improvements to the road through North Wales to Holyhead which Telford masterminded between 1815 and 1826. Parker credited the new road with increasing prosperity along its route: 'the grand Irish road seems to shed fertility upon its neighbourhood, and there do I see woodland or meadow scenery for elsewhere there are only barren mountains.'[21] Of more immediate benefit for travellers was the increased comfort and speed of coaches, which resulted in significantly shorter travel times. In 1815, the mail coach from Holyhead to Shrewsbury took seventeen hours, by 1827 this was reduced to under twelve hours. Parker's accounts confirm these figures: in 1819 he 'left Oswestry 27 September at 7 oclock, Capel cerig between 3 and 4', a journey of over eight hours to cover just 50 miles. In 1832, the same journey but on the more expensive mail coach, which had priority and made fewer stops, took

The Wynnstay Hotel, Oswestry

only 5½ hours, including a break of 25 minutes at Corwen. Parker would travel as far as Betws-y-coed, Capel Curig, Llanberis or Bangor depending on which part of Snowdonia he intended to explore.

The Holyhead Road Commission, the body set up by parliament in 1815 to undertake the improvement of the road, agreed in 1818 to take over the section of route belonging to the Oswestry Turnpike Trustees on condition that it would continue to go through the centre of the town. This meant that stagecoaches stopped at the Wynnstay Arms, the town's principal inn, which had been built in the 1790s by Sir Watkin Williams Wynn, where Parker's journeys began. Two documents, both from 1818 (when negotiations between the local turnpike trust and the new commission were in progress) illustrate the significance that the 'Irish Road' had for the town and its prosperity. The first is a plan on which is marked the route traffic would take through Oswestry and the second advertises the distances between the various 'stages' on the route to Holyhead.

Travel by any means other than on foot was expensive and beyond the reach of most of the population. Coach fares varied – travelling inside on a mail coach was the most expensive: in 1832, Parker paid £1-5-0 (one pound, five shillings) from Capel Curig to Oswestry and, in addition, he tipped the coachman and the guard a generous 4/- (four shillings). In contrast, the journey from Oswestry travelling 'outside' – on the roof of the coach exposed to the weather – was only 13/- (thirteen shillings).[22] The horses were changed at the towns en route, which were usually some twelve or so miles apart. This took only a few minutes but longer stops for refreshment were made at the larger inns and hotels. Parker seems to have eaten less frequently than his fellow passengers. In September 1831, 'at Llangollen while coach breakfasted went up to and saw Miss Ponsonby.' Sarah Ponsonby and Lady Eleanor Butler, the Ladies of Llangollen, had since 1780 made their home at Plas Newydd, just above the town and, until Sarah's death in 1831, received hundreds of visitors, including many of the most famous political and literary figures of the time. But Parker had a closer connection than most as for many years his mother had been a friend and correspondent of Sarah Ponsonby. In July 1831, she wrote inviting Mrs Parker to come to see a bed of pinks in her garden 'which I think you would like to see and *inhale*'. Mary Parker, John's sister, had surreptitiously made a drawing of the two ladies in 1828. Eleanor Butler had died in June 1831 and, when Parker called in September 1831, Sarah Ponsonby had only three months to live, so he must have been one of her last visitors.

On another journey in 1832, while most passengers dined at Corwen, he 'made a vignette [a drawing] of the church and examined what is said to be the mark of Glyndwr's dagger on the S[outh] side of the chancel'. One of his few references to food on a journey occurs in 1822, when he commented on 'the fruit woman who attended the coach while changing horses at Betws y

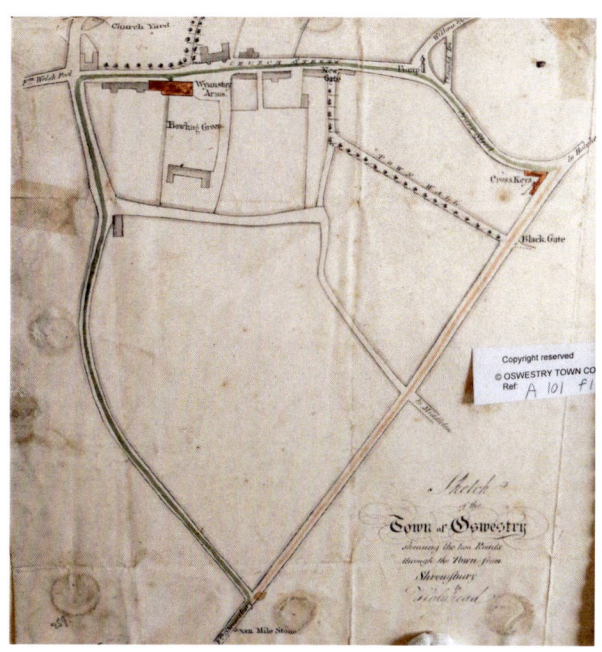

Plan of Oswestry dated 1818, showing the route taken by
stagecoaches travelling between London and Holyhead
by permission of Oswestry Town Council archives

A correct Table of the Stages between Oswestry and London
and the distances between Oswestry and Holyhead
by permission of Oswestry Town Council archives

47

coed [and] offered us plenty of green gages, which I do not think are yet ripe in England.'

Parker records only one accident and that involved a carriage on the Beddgelert road, which delayed *The Snowdonian* coach in July 1833, enabling him to catch it. But he could not escape the perennial inconveniences which plagued travellers. On his second visit to Capel Curig in the summer of 1832, he discovered that 'my carpet bag [was] left behind by the Guard at Corwen – he also left some luggage belonging to another passenger there.' He had 'only the clothes on my back' and 'a travelling desk, of which the key is in my bag!' Mr Clarke the innkeeper arranged for a note to go back to Corwen with the mail coach and, on the next afternoon, *The Snowdonian* delivered the bag to Capel Curig.

Parker's journeys in the 1820s and 1830s saw the heyday of the coaching era before the railways arrived in North Wales; the line from Chester to Holyhead was completed with the building of the Britannia Bridge over the Menai Strait in 1850. The following decade saw lines linking most of the popular tourist centres, but there

The Ladies of Llangollen, engraving by R.J. Lane from a drawing by Lady Leighton

remained a gap between Corwen and Betws-y-coed which had to be crossed by coach, by gig, on horseback or on foot. Parker's painting of *Pengwrdd* [sic] *an Ale House between Capel Curig and Beddgelert, 21 July 1832* shows the sort of accommodation available before the building of more comfortable hotels which the establishment of regular coach services and the increasing number of tourists encouraged.

The improvements in roads and inns are neatly summed up by Parker in 1831 when he noted the 'Inn lately built at the very foot of the mountain [Snowdon] – it is called Pen Gwryd; the new road through the Pass of Llanberis, opened about 3 weeks ago and a coach called the Snowdonian goes on Tuesdays, Thursdays and Saturdays from Carnarvon to Capel cerig'. An earlier improvement was the new road built by Lord Penrhyn from Bangor to Capel Curig, where he commissioned Benjamin Wyatt to design an inn which was open by 1801, and it was here that Parker stayed most frequently.

The largest of the new hotels was the Penrhyn Arms at Bangor. In 1830, Thomas Coleman noted that 'the Penrhyn Arms make up one hundred beds when necessary and there were 99 the night we went there and we filled the only remaining bed.' In his opinion, it

'Pengwrdd, An Ale house between Capel Curig and Beddgelert, 21 July 1832'

was 'a most magnificent hotel ... admirably managed'.[23] Beaumaris was another town which benefitted from the influx of tourists into North Wales. Here too an aristocratic local landowner led the way; in 1805–06, Viscount Bulkeley sponsored the building of a road from Menai Bridge to Beaumaris in anticipation of the construction of a bridge across the Strait. Twenty years later, Telford's bridge was opened and Beaumaris soon acquired the trappings of a fashionable resort. The Bulkeley Arms Hotel, begun in 1830, was where Parker enjoyed his stay three years later, by which time the magnificent Victoria Terrace, built in classical style and facing the Menai Strait, was complete. Such were the economic and social changes introduced by the growth of faster, more comfortable links between North Wales and the rest of the country.

Parker did not keep detailed accounts of what he spent on accommodation, limiting himself to occasional notes. For example, in June 1832, he paid £1-12-8 for three days' accommodation with meals, of which 7 shillings was for gratuities to the staff, including 3/6 for the 'chambermaid [and] washing'. On his more extensive tour of Snowdonia in 1833, he 'settled [the] bill for rather more than 9 days at Capel cerig – charges reasonable, breakfast 2s dinner 2s 6d, wine ½ pint sherry, 1s 6d coffee 1s 6d, Bed 2s'. However, he was angry at what he considered 'exorbitant charges' at the Castle Hotel in Conwy in 1828 ('will try to avoid going back'),

Capel Curig Hotel, from *Stereographs* by Francis Bedford, no. 128, the Michael Freeman Collection

The Sportsman Hotel, Castle Street, Caernarfon, 1850, engraving by W. Wood, Welsh Landscape Collection, LlGC/NLW

but at Llanrwst the charges were 'moderate', with 'bed a shilling a night, Breakfast 1s 3d, dinner 2s'.

Sometimes the food prompted comments. At Llanberis in July 1832, he 'had some excellent mutton for supper and some good rum which when mixed with water & sugar I found a pleasant substitute for wine'. But at Pen y Gwryd, there was 'nothing to be had for dinner except bacon and eggs and a few infant fishes too small to be eaten. They had however some whiskey and good ale.' On his visit to Llŷn in 1829, he stayed at the rectory in Llanengan, where he had a bad cold which meant he had 'breakfast in bed; unwell all day, white wine, whey and nitre again'. (Nitrates were used to treat angina and other disorders.)

Like many visitors he was impressed by Welsh harpists. When Parker and Neave stayed at The Goat in Caernarfon, 'in the evening we sent for Richard Davies, [who] played the Overture in Samson almost all through without more than a trifling deviation from the very notes of the original.' In *The Passengers*, his three travellers were entertained by 'Evan Jones, the harper … [with] a succession of elegant Welsh airs, played in a passage leading to the parlour. We cannot think of any thing else that peculiarly distinguished this repast from what an English inn of the same stamp would furnish.' Later, one of his friends asks Clanvoy, 'What air is the harper playing?' The answer is '"Nos Galan" (New-Year's Night); a fine, solemn, stanzaic melody; perhaps Druidic in its origin: at all events, of great antiquity.' For Parker, the druids were never far away.

As an artist, he was very appreciative of the views from hotels. At Capel Curig, he had a bedroom which looked across to Moel Siabod so, when it rained the day after he arrived, he was able to sketch the mountain from the window. At the Bulkeley Arms in Beaumaris, 'The view of Snowdonia from the coffee room is most

Penrhyn Arms Hotel, c. 1840 W.L. Cole,
Welsh Landscape Collection, LlGC/NLW

View from the Hotel at Bangor, N. Wales, Charlotte Canning
by permission of the Royal Collection Trust

Victoria Terrace, Beaumaris

enchanting.' The Penrhyn Arms at Bangor offered a view worthy of the words of Ajax on the coast of the Troad, the site of Troy: 'Oh, the roaring sea-ways, and the caves along the shore, and the grove on the headland.'[24]

The large number of tourists meant that Parker sometimes found difficulty getting a place on a coach or a bed for the night. In June 1826, he had 'intended taking the coach from Betws y coed to Capel cerig but the two coaches that passed were full inside and outside'. Six years later, he 'Stopped at the Dolbadarn Inn after passing a new but unfinished Inn, building by Mr Asheton Smith.' (The Assheton-Smith family owned the Dinorwic slate quarries, and built the Royal Victoria Hotel at Llanberis, which opened in 1832.) 'It will contain 26 best bedrooms. The Dolbadarn Inn was also full! And here I met Mr Dugmore again who was unable to get a bed. This mishap sent me off course against my will to Carnarvon, 8 miles from Dolbadarn and 18 from Capel cerig.' On his return journey from Capel Curig to Oswestry, he caught the express coach and was 'fortunate in getting a place at all, still more so in securing an inside one', which was just as well as it rained most of the way.

By the early 1830s, the rush of visitors to Wales was prompting some writers to complain in terms that sound very familiar today – about the deleterious effects of tourism. In 1832, an anonymous contributor to the *Cambrian Quarterly Magazine & Celtic Repertory* bemoaned the changes that were happening. 'The lowly retreats of shepherds are no sooner made the headquarters of summer visitants than they cease to be lovely. The livery servants, the lady's maids, the grooms, and jockies [sic], that dog the heels of shooting or racing gentlemen, transfigure a sweet rustic village in a surprisingly short time. Hotels start up, London suburban boxes, with sashes and knockers, and staring shops, startle the pensive traveller at his twilight hoped-for place of rest; drunkenness and midnight ranting of songs and revels banish owls and cuckoos, he finds "Cockney land is opened in the wild." Certain it is, that whoever desires to see Welsh life, such as lord Littleton saw and admired, and described in 1754, must, of all places shun those to which the titled tourist has drawn the tide of fashionable resort by his enthusiastic description. For this reason these our travellers are not fashionable ones, but plain lowly men, stealing humbly and simply into those scenes, the very essence of whose charms is lowliness and simplicity.'[25] While he appreciated the improvements made to travel and accommodation, Parker would have agreed with this disillusioned visitor which is why so many of his walks took him to secluded and unfrequented parts of Snowdonia.

[20] Ian Mortimer's *The Time Traveller's Guide to Regency Britain* 2020 covers the period 1789 to 1830 and provides a very readable introduction to everyday life during the first half of Parker's lifetime. The chapters on 'Travelling' and 'Where to Stay' are particularly relevant.

[21] Jamie Quartermaine, Barrie Trinder and Rick Turner, *Thomas Telford's Holyhead Road: The A5 in north Wales* The Council for British Archaeology, 2003, explains how Telford altered and improved the road through Snowdonia and gives much useful information about the practicalities of travel.

[22] In pre-decimal currency there were 12 pence to a shilling and 20 shillings to the pound; I have left the figures as Parker wrote them rather than convert them to decimal values. To give some idea of the value of what he paid, a comparison with the wages of farm labourers, the largest group of workers in the country at the time, is more useful than a multiplier. In 1832, a nationwide review of agricultural labourers' wages revealed that their wages varied between 9 and 12 shillings per week.

[23] Thomas Coleman, 'Journal of a Tour into north Wales with Mrs Coleman', NLW Minor Deposit, 1544, ff. 12–13, 27.

[24] From a chorus in Sophocles' *Ajax*; thanks to David Morgan for the translation of Parker's original Greek quotation.

[25] Anon, 'Conversations of poets among the Mountains', *Cambrian Quarterly & Celtic Repository,* Vol. 1V, No. 16 (October 1832), 433–455. Lord George Lyttleton, 1709–73, wrote letters about Snowdon in 1756 but they were not published until 1774.

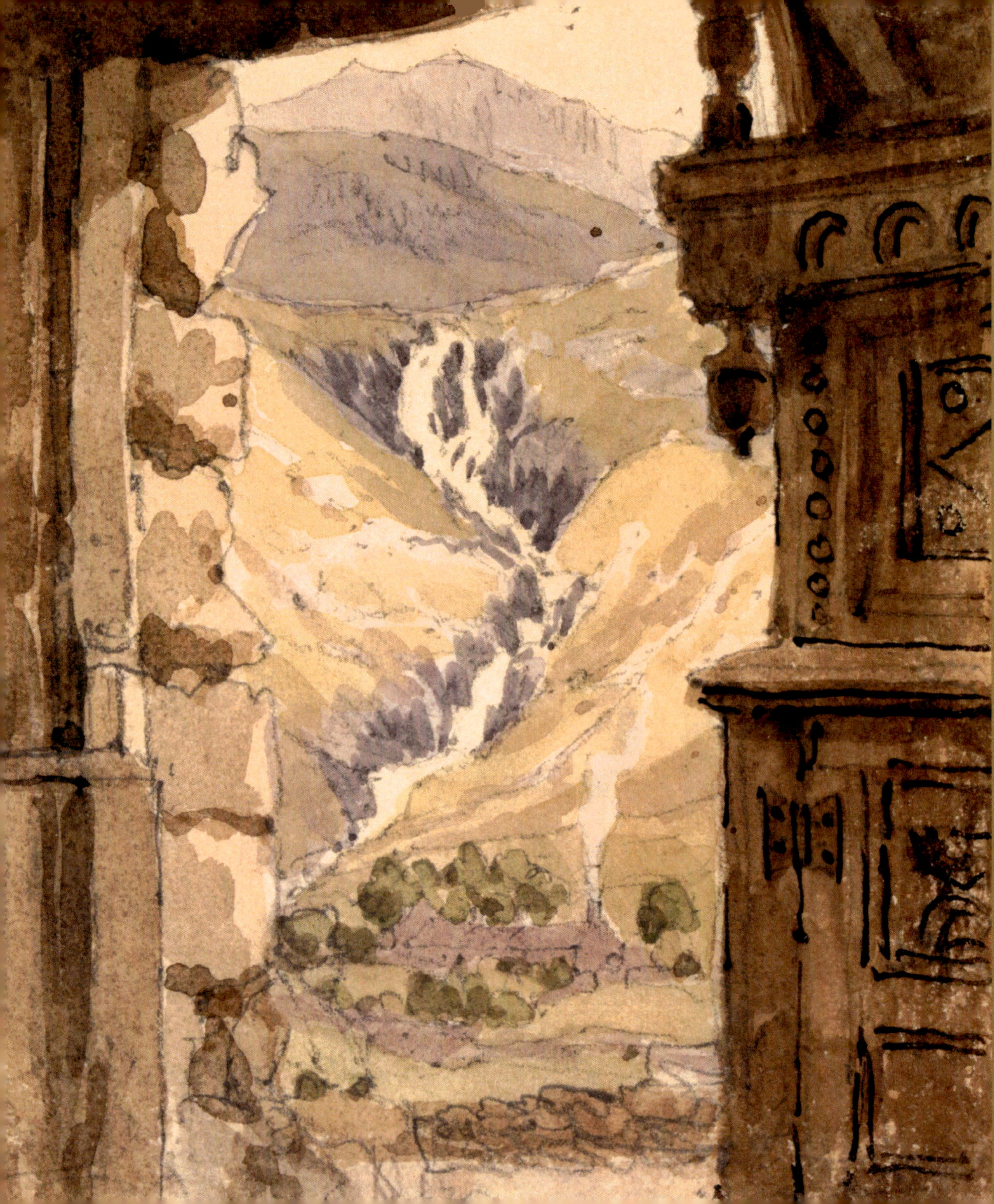

Chapter Six
Walking with Parker

'View from doorway of cottage in Cwm Dyli
called Gwastad Annas, September 1831'

Once settled at an inn, Parker planned his expeditions, which were sometimes determined by the weather, particularly if he proposed to climb one of the peaks. He used the extensive coach service for journeys to neighbouring towns and to places he wished to sketch. On 20 June 1833, while out walking, he was 'overtaken on [the] road by Wonder coach and went outside for 4½ miles, gave the coachman 1s 6d, alighted at Benglog falls' [Rhaeadr Ogwen or Ogwen Falls]. Two days later, after an early dinner, he again caught The Wonder to the falls, then discovered he had left his sketching pencil behind but was able to borrow one from the guard on the coach, on which 'I am to return on Monday'. Like his alter ego Clanvoy in The Passengers, Parker was well known to the coachmen on the Irish Road.

When the Parker family stayed at Bodowen, near Barmouth, visits were made either on horseback or in 'a car with my uncle's horse', which carried his mother and two sisters, Mary and Elizabeth. For journeys which allowed him more freedom, he hired a horse or took a gig or a chaise, a light two-wheeled vehicle pulled by one horse, which could be hired from an inn, either with a driver or post-boy or driven himself. In 1820 Parker recorded, 'Next day chaise to Caernarvon; dismissed the Post Boy at the Goat inn went to the castle.' When he visited Pwllheli, where the coach service terminated, he hired 'a car and horse for two days for 15s; over the sand to Llanbedrog'. Here Parker paid well below the usual price for a chaise; a fee of a guinea a day was common. On his Welsh tour in 1846, Parker took his own gig from Llanyblodwel, through Llangynog to Bala, which involved going over a pass at 1,650 feet.

In 1819, he had a rather unsettling ride from Beddgelert to Llanberis on a hired pony: 'I was riding through rather boggy ground and my pony stopped short. I whipped him on, but in an instant found him sinking under me in a green morass. I leapt off and reached the other side, for it was not many feet wide and lugged out the poor pony struggling with his terror, and accusing me with his eyes in quite a moving manner. We at last were both on the other side, minus a stirrup and a glove which may reward antiquarian researches when this morass is explored.' On a ride from Bodowen, his horse Mazeppa was stung under the tail by a gadfly.

Of course much of Parker's exploration took him to remote places well away from roads or tracks and he spent many hours in Snowdonia on foot. He climbed all the well-known peaks – Snowdon, Moel Siabod, Lliwedd, the Glyderau – and he was also an avid explorer of lakes and 'cascades' or waterfalls. Sometimes he had company on his travels. The tours of 1819 and 1820 were made with school friends; the first with Charles T. Corydon Luxmoore and on the second he was accompanied 'by my friend Neave'. The European tour in 1827 was a family affair with his mother, brother and sister but otherwise he travelled alone except when he took a servant. In 1832, when he went to St Asaph, he 'left Sweeney in [the] gig with Edward about 11 oclock'. In 1846, 'At Llanuwchllyn I put up the horse and Evan went in search of a fishing party who had carried off my umbrella instead of their own.' Occasionally he hired a guide, as in 1832 when he went 'to the Poetmaking stone'.

Parker seems to have got on well with the wide variety of people he met on his tours through Wales. He enjoyed unexpected meetings on the road or at the inns and hotels where he stayed. In 1819, he records dining with 'Captain Grey of the army office' at Capel Curig and walking with him to the foot of Glyder Fach. He joined 'the Townshend party and drank tea with them' at the Capel Curig inn in 1822 and then bumped into Cory Luxmoore and his wife and two sisters. The following year, he enjoyed the company of 'a German party' – one gentleman and two ladies he met at Beddgelert – and he had 'a good deal of very pleasant conversation with him'. He met 'Mr Barnaby of Worcester, lately a curate of Oswestry' in July 1832, at the Dolbadarn inn; he had walked 18 miles over the hills from Ffestiniog. The two energetic clerics walked together for three miles and, when they parted, Parker gave Barnaby a sketch of the route to follow on the rest of his walk.

The next year, he joined a Mr Darwell and two friends on their walk towards Llanberis, where he left them to go sketching. 'They were Cambridge men, well known to Professor Sedgwick' who had been in North Wales during the past two summers. Sedgwick was an Anglican clergyman better known as 'the father of British geology'. According to Parker's companions, Sedgwick found 'Snowdonia to be extremely perplexing as to Geology'. Parker met Sedgwick himself in 1846 at Mallwyd, where he gave the geologist a lift in his gig to Dinas Mawddwy. When they parted, Parker realised that he still had the professor's geological hammer, so hastily turned back to return 'the valued implement... to its owner'. Sedgwick was accompanied by an assistant 'whose name is Ruthven, of whose attainments and experience the professor spoke highly'. John Ruthven (1793–1868) was an amateur geologist — he earned his living as a cobbler in Kendal — who made important contributions to the geology of the Lake District. A week after his conversation about geology, Parker found further company at the hotel: 'On entering the coffee room at Capel cerig [sic] I found Dryden Corbett and 3 other men, one a great traveller full of conversation.'

In 1820, he and Neave climbed Snowdon at night – the first section on ponies – to see the dawn, something which Romantic young men felt impelled to experience. They started from Llyn 'Cwellyn' and then followed 'the miners' road' and near the summit they sent the ponies back to Llanberis. 'Splendid sunrise. Went to sleep below the summit but woken by shepherds and dogs who were watching the progress of a pack of foxhounds (ten couple) along the Bwlch Saethau.'

On many of his walks Parker was far from an inn or hotel where he could find refreshment, so he took supplies with him and on occasion called at cottages to ask for a drink. During one hike in 1819 he and his companion were sustained by 'cheese, Ale and the finest bread we ever tasted'. On 3 July 1823, he left Beddgelert, walked, sketched and stopped for water at a cottage where, 'They gave me a bowl of buttermilk part of which I drank and returned the rest with a remnant of my sandwiches.' In 1826, the coach dropped him at Betws-y-coed 'at about half after twelve; ordered sandwiches then set out with a view to reach the Llydir [Lledr]'. He mentions drinking brandy with water from streams on several occasions. On a hot day walking in the Arran mountains with his servant in 1846, 'We trudged along under a broiling sun', found some fresh water which 'when mixed with a little brandy will do no harm, though taken in a state of profuse perspiration if at least the exercise be continued afterwards' – not something a modern walker would advise.

On a walk to Llyn Geirionydd in June 1833, he was caught in a storm and got drenched; he sought refuge in a cottage and recorded his generous welcome. The mistress 'busied herself in preparing a meal and lighting a peat fire to dry my shoes. A glass of rum was produced and another poured into a basin of warm milk & sugar. A large oatmeal cake made its appearance with butter and curds and some cakes were broiled on the hearth. The good lady was also getting ready some tea (black and green) which however I declined; in short there was no lack of provision or welcome in this cottage. Had it not been for this timely refreshment I should probably have caught a dangerous cold, for not having intended, when I left Capel cerig, to go so far, I had no spirits to mix with water at the mountain torrents and had only a dry luncheon of egg sandwich. Laying my wet feet upon the turf and placing my shoes in such a position as to admit the sun which partially dried them. At half past 5 I left this house of entertainment, and partly from not having smaller silver and partly from a wish to reward attentions to a lonely tourist I gave her two shillings.' This is one of the few examples of a tourist describing the food of the people of Snowdonia, and the only time Parker recounted a visit to a cottage rather than a hotel or a gentry house. He did paint a small picture entitled View from doorway of cottage in Cwm Dyli called Gwastad Annas September 1831. This shows, to the left of the doorway, part of an ornate piece of furniture which might be a 'tridarn', a three stage dresser particularly associated with Snowdonia. In 1829, when he was in Llŷn looking for accommodation, he found at the inn in Abersoch a 'singular bedroom open at the top to all the rest of the house'. This sounds like a croglofft, where the bedroom is on a platform which covers only half of the ground floor.

The Llyn Geirionydd walk had a special significance for Parker because of its associations with two of the famous Welsh bards of the later sixth-century, Aneirin and Taliesin. In Parker's eyes, Snowdonia was inhabited by the shades of legendary figures from the distant – and often very obscure – past. In The Passengers, he extolled the talents and works of such poets to his companions and he liked to see similarities between them and the Classical authors he had studied at school. The area around Llyn Geirionydd was 'frequented by the inventor of Welch metre, by one to whom classical versification was not unknown'. This is a reference to Aneirin, whose fame was recorded by Taliesin, who lived on the shores of Llyn Geirionydd, and 'I felt anxious to examine the scene on which the eyes of that great poet so frequently rested.' However, Parker had to admit that, 'The neighbourhood of Taliesin's abode was I am sorry to say less interesting than I could have desired'; though perhaps his disappointment was coloured by the gale which was still raging. He noted that, 'The ruins of the house are said to be still in existence' but 'unless they are those contiguous to the cottage of Hafod y Rhiw I could perceive no other vestige of an ancient building'. This shows Parker's poetic wish-fulfilment – sixth-century houses survived only in his imagination.

All these journeys to the heartland of Welsh-speaking Wales raise the question: how much Welsh could Parker speak or understand? The majority of the tourists who came to Wales at this time were English and unable to speak much, if any, Welsh. In 1838, Thomas Roberts of Pwllheli published The Welsh Interpreter, advertised as 'a collection of useful and familiar phrases' for visitors who 'may wish to make themselves understood by the peasantry during their rambles through Wales'. The appearance of the book suggests that some of the tourists were willing to attempt limited conversations with local people. Parker was in many respects an Englishman typical of his time and class, but he lived almost all his life in Wales or close to the border and he spent most of his time away from home travelling in Wales. In Llanmyrewig, Parker would probably not have heard much Welsh spoken, the area around Newtown was one of the more Anglicised parts of the country. When he travelled in North Wales, he paid very careful attention to the Welsh names for mountains, streams, lakes and other features in the landscape. There is no evidence that he spoke much Welsh but he was keen to understand what the names meant. He appreciated the descriptive names such as Llyn Myngli ('the lake of the shallow shore') and on the Arrans he noted 'Llaethnant, means milky brook, Cwm Derwyn, Oak Hollow.' Parker often refers to Snowdon as Wyddfa and on occasion 'Eruri' (Eryri) – Welsh names for the mountain and the area of Snowdonia. He followed contemporary usage in writing 'v' for 'f' in place names such as Clynnog Fawr and Pentrefoelas and in the anglicised spelling of town names – Carnarvon, Conway, Dolgelly.[26]

How well he pronounced the words we can't tell, but in The Passengers he explained to his companions that 'Rheeg which they spell in the Welsh way Rûg' and that Dolwyddelan was pronounced Dōlwyddèlan. He did admit that 'a mountain called the Cnicht [is] of difficult pronunciation'; however, when he came across a sheep trapped on the rocks at Rhaeadr Cwm Dyli, a cascade on the lower part of Snowdon, he was able to explain the location to shepherds he met later. On Sunday, July 1st 1832, when staying at Llanberis, he was told that Mr Hughes, the local clergyman, was ill and was asked, by a waiter at the hotel, if he would preach the sermon. Parker said he could not preach in Welsh but he did so in English and 'the congregation appeared attentive'. That he was asked suggests it was assumed he had some knowledge of the language.

One modern Welsh place name prompted a furious outburst. In August 1847, Parker stayed at the Castle Hotel 'in a large village near the slate quarries, the real name of it is Tregrispil, but as that seemed odd and barbarous they have named it from a great Congregationalist meeting house called Bethesda, which in prominent ugliness even exceeds the Calvinistic Methodist chapel, its near neighbour. So this new and populous village has been called Bethesda, in defiance of all good taste and propriety. No doubt the proper name of this place would be Coitmore or Coedmawr, from the adjoining bridge and ruined castle, both of which bear that name, the latter having some record in history.'[27]

---

[26] The subject of Welsh place names is a minefield, and recent changes to long-established place names have been controversial. Perrin points to the 'colonialist' influence of the Ordnance Survey in distorting Welsh names in Snowdonia. For an authoritative guide to the origins and meaning of Welsh place-names, the reader is advised to consult Hywel Wyn Owen and Richard Morgan, *The Dictionary of the Place-Names of Wales* Gomer, 2007. I have retained Parker's spelling of Caernarfon ('Carnarvon') and Conwy ('Conway') in contemporary references to those places.

[27] Where Parker found his alternative names is unclear; *The Dictionary of the Place-Names of Wales* gives an early name as Y Wern Uchaf.

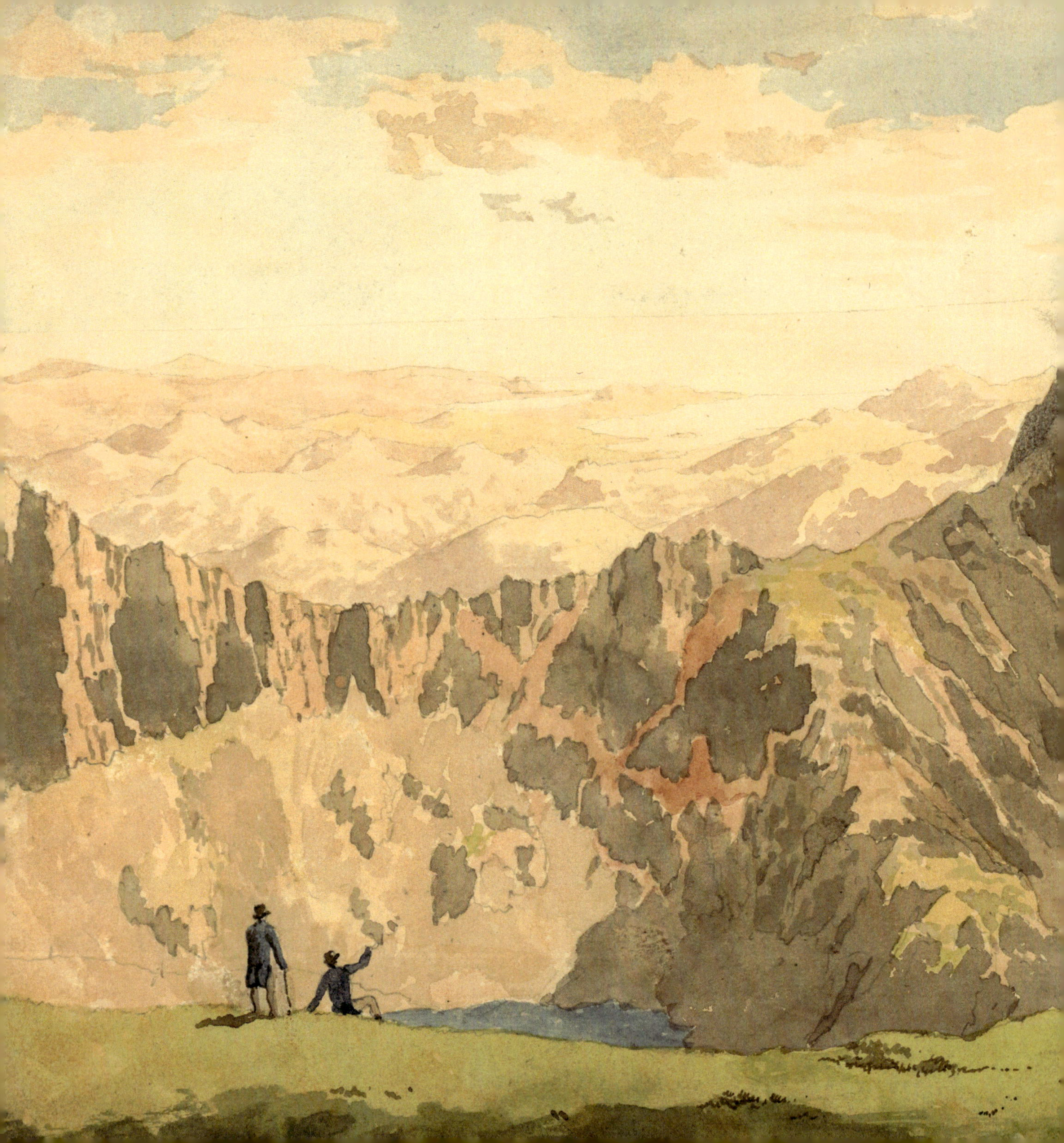

Chapter Seven
Exploring the landscape

Snowdon

MOUNTAINS

The tour he made with his family in 1827 included visits to sites in Switzerland that were already favourite destinations for British travellers. Chamonix offered the most spectacular views of Mont Blanc and Les Aiguilles and nearby was the immense glacier Le Mer de Glace. According to Parker, these sights were 'discovered' about eighty years previously by two Englishmen, Pococke and Windham, and he took a patriotic pride in 'the record of his countrymen who have never lost the reputation of being the first to explore unknown regions'. Richard Pococke was bishop of two Irish dioceses but an inveterate traveller, while William Windham was from a family of Norfolk landowners but lived in Geneva from 1740 to 1742.

Parker was suitably impressed by the 'incredibly magnificent scenery' with its 'glittering summits' and he made lots of sketches which he later coloured. But for him, Snowdonia's beauty excelled all other landscapes whether in the Lakes, Scotland, Ireland or the Alps. This appreciation was closely connected with his highly romanticised view of the history of North Wales; for him, this was the country of bards and poets, knights and warriors, myth and legend. In June 1820, he explained the superior attraction of Wales over Switzerland: 'Wales has been the favourite resort of music and poetry, while Switzerland, tho it may have given birth to great splendor [sic] of imagination in foreigners, has never been considered as a country whose native inhabitants are strongly endowed with either the one or the other ... The scenery of Wales [is] more ceremonious than that of Switzerland. The colouring altho occasionally splendid and contrasted beyond all description is yet in general of a softer and more tender kind. It is wild sweetness that prevails throughout. Add to this also the sweetness and poetic strength of the welch [sic] language, and the whole train of splendid or affecting recollections which history authenticates.'

Parker toured Ireland and Scotland and made beautiful paintings of the landscapes and he had to admit that 'Irish and Scotch lake scenery far surpasses this [Snowdonia] in extent of water and islands, of which in Wales there are so very few' but 'in its upper outlines this district is unrivalled. After becoming familiar with it, all other mountains look flat and tame.' The Lake

'Mer de Glace'

'Ullswater from Patterdale, July 22, 1825'

District, which he explored in 1825, offered magnificent mountain views but lacked that magic which he found in Snowdonia. 'In Wales the recollections of History, the splendour of poetical talents adorning the dark ages, and the sufferings of a conquered nation, give to the landscape an interest ... that few other places could afford. The character of the scenery sustains and elevates this interest for it is wild, awful, and of a more severe style than any part of the English lakes.' The Lakes 'do not abound in legendary lore. A few traces of past ages are swallowed up in the joyous aspect of modern civilization. There are no ruins. These vallies [sic], these mountains have never echoed the shout of triumph or the wailing of despair ... the charm of historical interest is not here, it is a kind of American beauty, resulting simply from present outward elegance, devoid of historical recollection.' Snowdonia, on the other hand, was rich in such echoes and memories. Here the lakes were the meeting places of fairies or they concealed monsters in their depths; heroes such as Arthur and Owain Glyndŵr had fought the Saeson (the Saxons, the English) in the mountains and hidden in caves from where they might one day return.

Parker felt some observations on mountain scenery were grossly overwrought. For example, the road through Penmaenmawr to Conwy, 'which some travellers say requires a superhuman courage to pass, the absurd descriptions of it surpass imagination, bombastic epithets'. In his journals, Parker was more restrained, but not less moved by what he saw; his responses to the landscape were deeply felt but based on his close observation of nature. On his tour of 1819, the first he recorded in his journals, he declared 'The style of this country [Snowdonia] is peculiarly fine... It might be called a School for painters.' Of walking down Moel Siabod, he wrote, 'I behold this mountain, unexpectedly and with pleasure. These grey cliffs, that almost overhung their bases, are at one moment glittering in the sunshine at another dark with passing shadows, below them I see desolation, indeed yet so adorn'd and animated by the fine weather, that it can hardly be called mournful.' And, at the end of this visit (in 1822), 'I leave Wales, as usual impressed with higher notions of its grandeur and beauty than I had before.' Two other mountains prompted feelings of awe; 'How princely, how superb is that alpine pyramid of Trevaen'

Two views of Snowdon, the one on the right shows the Miners' Track

and Cnicht he thought 'in its form extremely beautiful, and certainly the steepest mountain in North Wales.' But none could compete with Snowdon. In 1824 at Llyn Goch, 'The arms of Snowdon appear to embrace the traveller and he feels himself surrounded by the mountain.' Of Snowdon in a storm, he wrote, 'If ever there was a scene of dismal grandeur I saw it then.' He returns to the inn inspired by 'what I have seen today [which] excels all that I ever saw before as to subject for drawing'. On 13 August 1847, he walked to Nant Ffrancon, where he saw Snowdon 'cloudless, and calm, pale and serene, dim and remote, like some aerial vision'. Snowdon of all the mountains remained his favourite.

One of his most atmospheric paintings of mountains shows the view westwards from the Iron Age hillfort of Tre'r Ceiri on the north coast of the Llŷn Peninsula.[28] 'Remains of walls extensive, sloping to the Southwest, most perfect on the North & west, two entrances.' Typically, Parker found time at Tre'r Ceiri to investigate the flora and he was pleased to find 'a patch of the cup lichen in magnificent fructification, as if a whole stick of sealing wax had been melted and dropped over it'.

He was also enthusiastic about the scenery of the Mawddach estuary, which he came to know well during visits to Bodowen. In June 1820, he went with Neave 'Down the Mawddach estuary to Dolgelly; this is as beautiful as it is praised… It is in fact too beautiful to appear a real view, it is a vision.' In Parker's opinion, it made all other views seem 'mean and insignificant'. Later on this tour, he walked from Barmouth to see 'uncle Owen's cottage' [sic], Bodowen, which is 'beautifully situated and has a veranda [sic] on two sides of it'. He enjoyed the views from above the house, where there was 'wood, sea and mountain… in plenty… [which] formed glorious landscapes… I never had so completely so rich [a] foreground for so magnificent a prospect in the distance.'

In the landscape between Dolgellau and Ffestiniog, he found rugged and dramatic views for his paintings. He spent some days in May 1840 exploring Cadair Idris and also 'walked below Craig y deryn or Bird Rock'. In August 1846, he 'stopped at Pont Disynwy & made a careful sketch' on which the finished painting was based. On the same journey, he went to 'a public house on the upper Corwen road about 5 miles from Bala called the Boot. Here put up the horse and walked to Llyn Carini [Llyn Caer-Euni] – a fine water near which I got a very good view of the distant lake of Bala.' On the same tour, Parker decided to climb 'Arran Fowddy' [sic] on a hot day in August and reached the pass between Aran Fawddwy and Aran Benllyn which is 'called Rhiw y ddafad, Sheep's Bank … Great was the labour of surmounting this bank of the sheep!' Parker was now 47 years old and for the first time mentions that he found the climb tiring and had to pause three times 'for breath'. After descending the mountain, he sent Evan ahead to fetch the gig and they drove the seven miles back to Mallwyd by moonlight.

'Tre'r Ceiri'

Bodowen and the Mawddach estuary

'Cader Idris, Craigaderyn, Pont Dysynni, August 29, 1846'

'Lake of Bala'

'Summit of Arran'

WATER

Water, whether in lakes, estuaries or falls, entranced him. The sound of a mountain stream was 'the voice of the high born, half seen river [which] seemed like the murmur of subdued applause'. On another occasion at Llanfawr, near Bala, he described a fast flowing river as a 'brawling torrent'. In June 1820, after lunch at the Tal-y-bwlch inn, he went with a guide to Rhaeadr Du, a waterfall on the Cynfael river near Ffestiniog (not to be confused with the better known Rhaeadr Du, near Ganllwyd twelve miles south of Ffestiniog). The falls 'I should suppose [are] as near perfection in point of beauty as the most fastidious artist could require.' Close by was Hugh Lloyd's pulpit – a column of rock in the middle of the fast-flowing river from which Hugh Lloyd, a local poet, astrologer and magician in the seventeenth-century, used to lead prayers and cast out devils and evil spirits. This was just the sort of mixture of myth and history that Parker loved but he did admit that 'presumably "his magic art" enabled him to get into this pulpit which is dangerously inaccessible'. Nearer home was Pistyll Rhaeadr, one of the Seven Wonders of Wales, which he visited and drew many times. Less well known was Pistyll Blaen y Cwm, where the infant Tanat river spills over the rocks and later flows at the bottom of the garden he created at the vicarage in Llanyblodwel.

Snowdonia's landscape, like the Lake District, is made memorable by the combination of mountains and water. Parker was familiar with the lakes around Snowdon, including the smaller, less well-known ones; he also sought out the lakes in less popular places. In June 1826, for example, west of Llanrwst, he explored Llyn Geirionydd, Llyn Bychan and Llyn Crafnant, the last of which 'with a few slight additions might rival any lake in Wales'; he then walked back past Gwydir Castle to the Cross Keys at Betws-y-coed. This was during a week when 'the continued heat of this weather is astonishing' and he bathed several times in the Afon Lledr between Betws and Dolwyddelan. In fact, he painted Llyn Crafnant with two men, one naked, by the side of the water; the painting is dated 21 June 1826. He also mentions bathing a number of times at Bodowen, where there was a ' bathing house'.

'Pistyll Blaen Cwm'

ROCKS

Parker was also fascinated by rocks. The landscape of the Severn Valley where his first parish was situated is one of gentle hills, with views eastwards towards the Breidden, and he drew and painted this many times, but when he went home to Sweeney Hall, he was close to

'A curious piece of rock ... near the Vale of Llansilin'

'The Bowder Stone, Borrowdale, July 23 1825'

'Craig y Rhiw'

'Rock strata Llangollen'

more exciting terrain. The limestone cliffs at Llanymynech and at Craig-y-rhiw, west of Oswestry, were among Parker's favourite places. On the road to Llangollen, the limestone edges which dominate the valley produced one of his most dramatic watercolours. The Lake District delighted him with its rocky landscape and in many paintings he placed rocks in the foreground; his view of Ullswater is a good example. Like many visitors he walked into Borrowdale to view and draw the Bowder Stone.

When he explored Snowdonia, he found even more dramatic falls of rock and mighty boulders and he wrote a memorandum, *'Observations upon rocks'*, in which he discussed their appeal.[29] The columns of vertical rocks 'stand ... in their lofty ranges, towering into the smooth sky, their serrated edges cutting sharply against the blue skylight of heaven [while] in the foreground, on the

'Rocks on Glyder Fach'

Maen Du, photograph by Trevor Littlewood

'Y Maen Du'

other hand they are lying like heaps of dead bodies after a battle, thrown head over heels, in every possible attitude and hideous mutilation.' The Glyderau were especially fascinating for their rock formations; Glyder Fawr he considered 'the richest view of rocky scenery that I have ever beheld'. He mused on the 'time, probably after the deluge, when the mountains were given to splitting and cracking then as they are now'. Sedgwick, the geologist, would have corrected these fantasies.

One particular stone had a special appeal, the rock known as 'the Poetmaking stone', Carreg y Bardd or Maen Du, sited below Clogwyn Du'r Arddu. He climbed on top of the rock, where 'lies a smaller stone finely poised which gives to the whole rock a druidical character'. He then spent a long time taking measurements and noting the presence of 'viviparous fescue, grass, white clover and bilberries'. For Parker, this stone epitomised the myths and stories which identified Snowdon as the Celtic Parnassus, the home of the Muses and thus of poetry, music and learning. A number of visitors to Snowdonia before Parker had repeated the story that anyone who slept a night on the mountain would awake a poet or a madman; however, he seems to have been the first to explore this particular site, record it in detail and identify it with a supernatural power. He later returned to 'this magnificent object', revised a former sketch and noted a fox earth below the stone. Maen Du for Parker was a place of myth, but worthy of accurate observation, both of its dimensions and its botanical specimens.

LLANBERIS PASS

Of all the places in Snowdonia in which he walked and painted, one was pre-eminent for Parker: the Llanberis Pass. In his Welsh Tours volume, between a detailed description of Eaton Hall in 1821 and his account of 'a

'Llanberis June 13 1860'

few days in North Wales 1822', he wrote a five page 'Description of the Pass of Llanberis'.³⁰

'This place has long been considered as the finest specimen of its kind that Wales possesses,' he writes. In Parker's eyes, the pass combined all the features of the landscape he most admired. On either side were majestic mountains – Glyder Fawr and Snowdon itself – while the slopes and the valley floor were strewn with rocks 'torn from their high situations, and thrown down, sometimes entire, and sometimes in small fragments over almost all the level space at the bottom'. Near Llanberis, there is a meadow fed by streams where 'the enclosed ground is ingrossed by the wild hyacinth which flowers in the month of July'. Halfway up the pass is 'an alpine pool called Ffynnon vrech (the spotted well)' where 'the rocks ... are overspread with an amazing variety of the rarest flowers, some of them sweetscented, and most of them very showy'. At the highest point, the traveller is rewarded with a 'prospect [that] includes the lakes of Llanberis, with the tower of Dolbadarn at their junction, the Menai Strait and Anglesey with Holyhead Mountain, while the nearer mountains on either side exhibit more variety of ruined precipice and rock, than could readily be found elsewhere.'

FLORA

Given his meticulous draughtsmanship and his love of the outdoors, it is not surprising that Parker made studies of flowers at Penarth and at the vicarage in Llanyblodwel, where he created a beautiful garden. When he went walking in the mountains, he was always on the lookout for unusual flowers and plants. In June 1820, he saw 'the roseroot (Abdiola rosca) [sic], the Snowdon pink, saxifrage; such plants in inaccessible places are protected from the rapacity and avarice of the seedsman and florist'. Three years later, he wrote, 'Wherever I go in Wales during the latter part of June I see and smell the butterfly orchis [sic]. High on the mountains, low in the vallies [sic] this beautiful flower is always within sight and in some places most abundant ... A very conspicuous vetch also spreads itself upon the sunny banks and ornaments the low grounds with particoloured blossoms of uncommon beauty.' During the same visit, he went to Nant Gwynant, where he 'passed high hayfields on a level with Pen [y] Gwryd, got back to the roadside where [I found] strawberries, white and red raspberries and the Tutsan or Park-leaves out of blossom.'

'Yellow Hellebore & withered oak leaves, February 1856'

'Specimens of the scarlet Perziza, from near old Red Pennarth Feb. 13 1830'

[28] Tre'r Ceiri ('the town of the giants') is one of the most spectacular historic sites in Britain. An Iron Age hillfort, but with stone – rather than the usual surviving earth – defences standing up to 4 metres high, and the remains of over a hundred stone huts inside the defensive walls.

[29] NLW MS18256C, pp 380–82.

[30] NLW MS 18256C, pp 85–90.

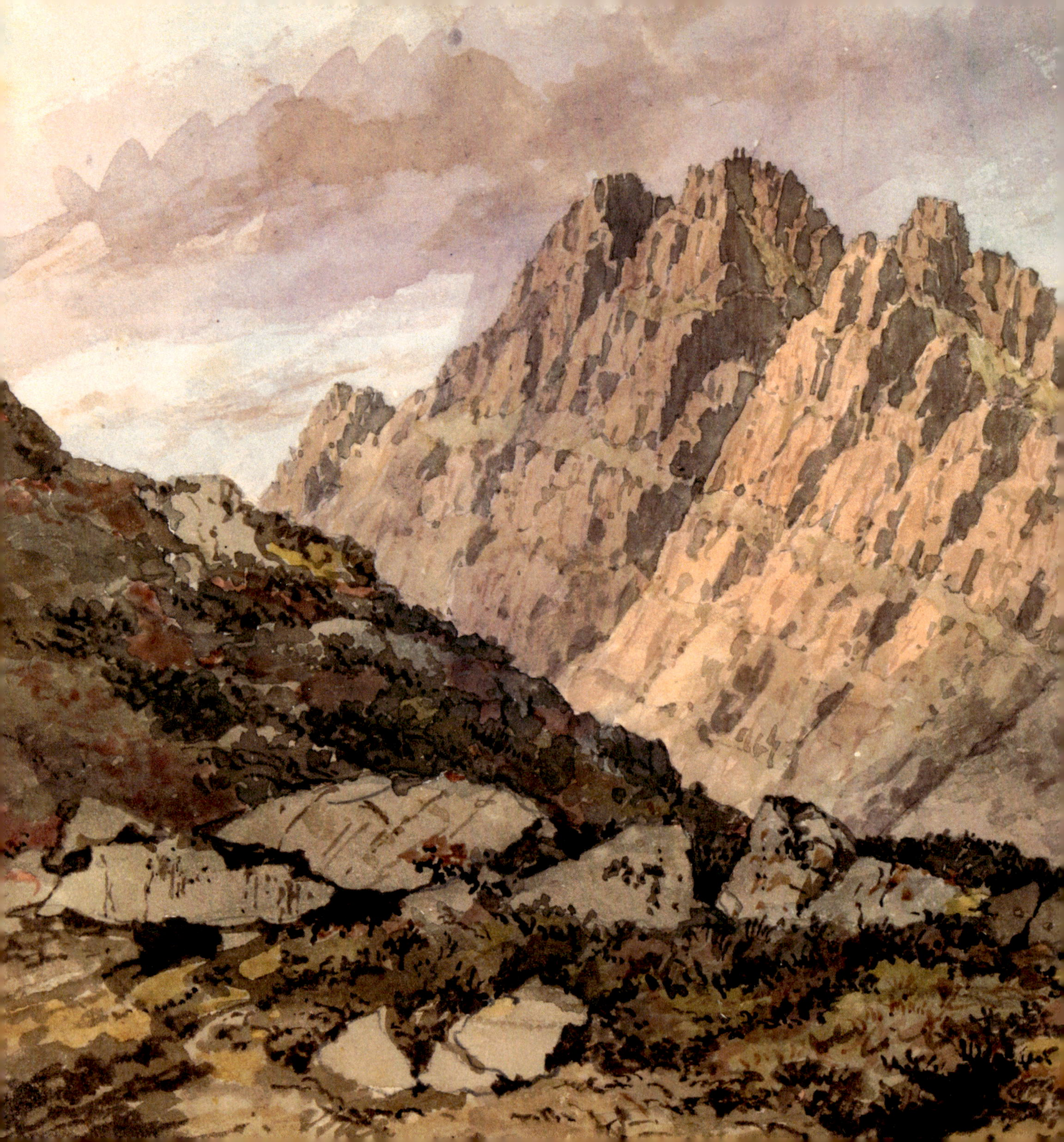

Chapter Eight
Parker the Artist

'Trewaen' [Tryfan]

John and his sister Mary were the first generation of a family which produced a succession of talented artists. Their elder brother Thomas, who died in 1833, also travelled widely, in northern Europe and Russia, with a professional artist, Silvestro Bossi, and Thomas himself made sketches of the Crimea. Mary, better known as an artist by her married name Lady Leighton, is today particularly remembered for her one published work – the depiction of the Ladies of Llangollen, Sarah Ponsonby and Lady Eleanor Butler, at tea in their library. This is based on drawings she made secretly as the Ladies are said to have forbidden anyone taking their portraits. A lithograph of Mary's drawing was produced by Richard James Lane in 1836.[31]

In addition Mary produced many volumes of portraits as well as albums of scenes from travels in the Holy Land. The National Library at Aberystwyth has three of her drawing volumes, one of which, *Snowdonia*, is a collection commemorating her brother, John. A second comprises portraits of Shropshire gentry neighbours and the third is a volume of views of Shropshire churches, an interest in ecclesiastical architecture she shared with her brother. Mary's daughter, Frances, inherited her mother's artistic talent and contributed some copies of her uncle's pictures for the commemorative volume. An unusual example of her artistic skill is preserved at Oberammergau in a large book showing scenes from the Passion play performed there.

The artistic lineage does not end with Frances; her brother, Stanley Leighton, left volumes of drawings of buildings, chiefly Shropshire houses. His interest in historic buildings led him to join the Society for the Protection of Ancient Buildings (SPAB), founded by William Morris, to protect buildings from overzealous restoration, which would have met with his uncle's enthusiastic approval.

As a schoolboy, Parker displayed considerable talent as a draughtsman and artist. At Eton he drew some of his friends and also buildings at the school and at Windsor. When he was at home from school he found architectural subjects in and around Shrewsbury. One of his early drawings – it is not dated but the signature suggests he did it as a teenager – is of the extraordinary house built by Richard Mytton at Garth, north of Welshpool.[32] A superb, flamboyant example of the early nineteenth-century Gothic style, Garth, completed in about 1812, no doubt captured the imagination of the schoolboy. The drawings of St Mary's church in Shrewsbury (dated 1811) and of the chapter house at Haughmond Abbey (1812) both show a command of perspective and an ability to record detailed architectural features accurately. At about the same time the young artist made a series of drawings of common birds which again show a precocious talent. He was also tackling landscapes. The dramatically coloured panorama of Snowdonia on page 42 is dated 1812, when John was 14. A pencil sketch of 'Snowden' – not dated but the misspelling and the signature show

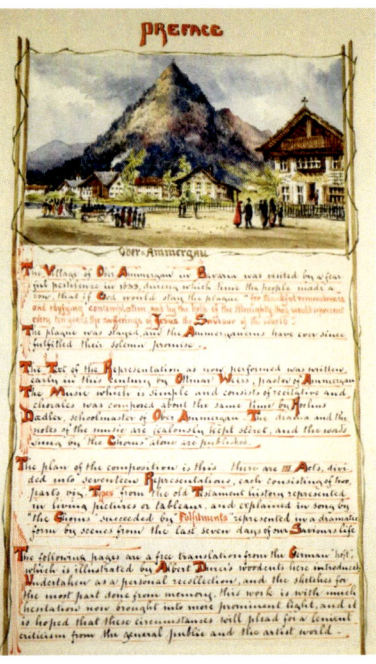

Travel Diary of Frances Christina Childe, The Community of Oberammergau archives

this to be an early work – displays a sweeping view of the mountains, with rocks in the foreground which was to be an important feature in his paintings. The impressive view of Llyn y Gader on the cover of this book was done when he was 19, but the depiction of the mountain and of the sky lacks the subtlety of Parker's later landscapes

Who taught Parker to draw and paint so skilfully? His siblings, Thomas and Mary, (he was a year younger than his brother and a year older than his sister), would no doubt have encouraged his early artistic efforts. There are interesting connections between Parker at Eton and a succession of teachers at the school. Three generations of the Evans family, originally from Flintshire, were 'drawing masters' at Eton. Samuel Evans occupied the post during Parker's time as a pupil and

'Shrewsbury'

'Chapter House at Haughmond Abbey 1812'

'Redwing from Nature, natural size, J P 6th December 1811'

'Garth, near Welshpool'

specialised in landscape painting. His son William, who was the same age as Parker and a fellow pupil, became much better known as an artist and exhibited his work, including views of Llanberis and Barmouth, in 1828 at the Royal Watercolour Society. (A third Evans, Samuel T. G. Evans, followed William as drawing master in 1877.) Given their Welsh origins and interest in the Welsh landscape it is very likely that the young Parker's enthusiasm for drawing and painting owed something to Samuel and John.[33]

Parker's drawings and paintings fall into four main groups: landscapes, churches and their furnishings, historic buildings and flora and fauna; he also filled many pages of drawing volumes with his designs for buildings, fonts, screens, pulpits and inscriptions, all of course in Gothic style. Judging by the number of subjects which are dated and can be ascribed to a particular journey, Parker drew rapidly. He usually sketched in pencil but sometimes he painted outdoors. On Tuesday June 19th 1820 he set off from Capel Curig 'for the base of Wythva', where he saw a field full of wild hyacinth 'which I sketched 'but they required the camel hair more than the Brookman's and Langdon's pencil'. (These pencils were particularly sought after by artists and writers; in 1818 Mary Shelley wrote from Rome asking Thomas Love Peacock to send her a dozen.[34]) Many of the drawings remain as pencil sketches, others he coloured when he was back at his hotel or much later, when he returned home. For example on September 2nd 1846, while staying in Bala, when he was 'sick and bilious this morning, coloured sketches indoors'. Some of his most appealing works are sketches made when he was a schoolboy and coloured much later, towards the end of his life: two drawings done in 1813 – of the Falls of Conway and of Pant y Glyn near Corwen – were coloured in 1858.

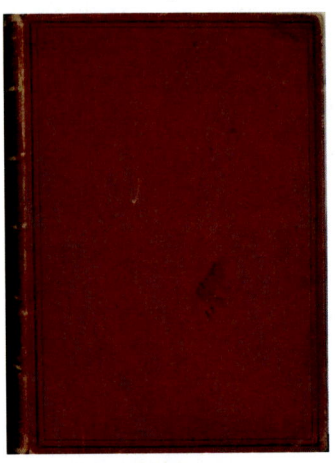

The Parker watercolours and sketches at the National Library number about 1200; the majority are in a series of more than 20 Drawing Volumes (all but two of which have been digitised and can be viewed online). The volumes measure approximately 20 by 14 inches; some pages show only one drawing or watercolour, but others have up to four pictures. A number of watercolours are mounted, including the series of Welsh Views many, of which are reproduced in this book. The paintings and drawings vary in size from between 4×7 to 9×11 inches. The details of architectural features and church furnishings are usually on a smaller scale as shown in the example from Drawing Volume 330.

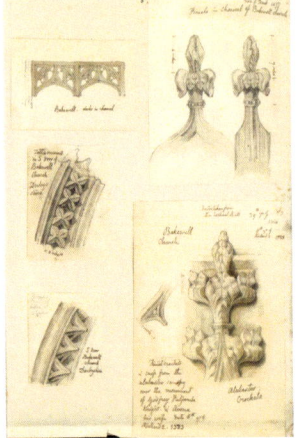

By the time Parker came to Snowdonia the area was already a mecca for artists attracted by its combination of mountains, lakes and waterfalls. Richard Wilson, born in Montgomeryshire, painted two views which became iconic images of north Wales: *'Snowdon from Llyn Nantlle'* (painted in 1765–6) and *'Cader Idris with Llyn-y-Cau'* (exhibited

Drawing Volume 330

A page from D.V. 330 showing details of Bakewell church, Derbyshire

'Snowden [sic] J.P.'

'Crib Goch from the grassy slope between it and crib y dystyll'

in 1774). It was the publication of engravings of Wilson's work, by John Boydell, in a set of six Welsh views in 1775, that established his enduring influence on contemporaries and later generations of landscape artits.[35] In May 1840 Parker walked up the eastern side of Cader Idris and reached the higher part of the mountain which 'equals almost anything on Snowdon but the rest of the mountain is much inferior'. He pressed on to find Wilson's 'noted view' but did not get 'near enough to ascertain whether it was idealized or not'.

A Welsh artist who made an important contribution to landscape painting was Thomas Jones of Pencerrig (1742–1803), but in his case the 'acceptance of what was presented to his eye [was] sufficient in itself'.[36] John 'Warwick' Smith (1749–1831), who had met Thomas Jones in Italy, made frequent visits to Wales between 1784 and 1806 and shared Parker's delight in the mountainous landscape and enthusiasm for historic buildings.[37] Thomas Pennant's *Journey to Snowdon* (1781) contained six plates depicting mountain views including 'Snowdon from Capel Cerig', 'A View in Nant Beris' and 'Dinas Emrys'. The illustrations were drawn by Moses Griffith under Pennant's supervision and they established those particular locations as the most popular destinations for subsequent generations of visiting artists.[38]

Where does John Parker fit into this succession of painters? He was familiar with the ideas of the Picturesque and wrote at some length about what constituted the elements which contributed to such scenes. The places which offered the best views were known to artists as 'stations' and were much frequented by tourists. In July 1832 Parker 'walked over the Glan y Bala grounds', in Llanberis, to 'my former station which is now spoiled by an unusual cause, the growing up of some oak trees', which presumably impeded his view of the mountains. At Llyn Geirionydd in June 1833, he admired the 'exceedingly grand' precipice rising from the lake, but 'the shores of this lake are not picturesque, there is now wood [land].'

But when he drew or painted Parker was influenced – like Thomas Jones – more by what he saw than the theories he discussed. He certainly appreciated the well-known views that Pennant and others had explored before him and some of his most impressive work captures the panoramas of Snowdon and Llanberis but

'Llyn Crafnant, 1826'

he also sought less familiar scenes such as Llyn Crafnant, Tre'r Ceiri, Maen Du and the rocky summit of Glyder Fach. Because he came so often to Snowdonia he drew some scenes many times; his drawing volumes show examples of simple pencil outlines, detailed sketches and watercolours, the latter showing a daring, and – for the period – unusual, use of colour.

Three examples of his landscapes – views of Tryfan, Y Cnicht and Llyn Crafnant – exhibit his particular qualities as an artist. Each of them reveals a close and accurate observation of mountains; the view of Tryfan is also informed by an awareness of geology which adds to its immediacy. His paintings show an understanding of those compositional elements which go to make a successful image: the majesty of Y Cnicht and Tryfan is emphasised by the detailed foreground in each case. Colour also plays an important part in the impact of his paintings. The use of different shades of blue at Llyn Crafnant – in the sky, the water and on the mountains – adds to the drama of the scene. Tryfan stands against a beautifully observed evening sky with its reflected light.

The inclusion of a nude in the painting of Llyn Crafnant is I believe, unique in landscape painting of Snowdonia in the early nineteenth-century. These prominently placed figures suggest a Classical source, which given Parker's education is unsurprising. The painting is described on the back as 'Llyn Crafnant and bathers 21 June 1826'. In his journal he records the heat of that week and bathing a number of times; he went to Llyn Crafnant on the 21st but does not mention bathing there, he did however include a sketch of the view in his journal and the comment, 'this is a hasty recollection of the subject.' No figures are included in the drawing.

In Peter Bishop's opinion 'accomplished watercolour painting such as we see in Parker's Welsh views suggests to me a fairly educated artist particularly in his construction of pictorial space and solid form [and] ... that he had some instruction on methods and materials by a more experienced practitioner.'[39] However apart from the influence of the Evanses at Eton I have found no evidence that Parker received instruction from any other artists. His innate ability and the sheer volume of his work suggests a man for whom drawing was a compulsion as well as a source of great fulfillment. The results are a series of landscapes which stand comparison with the work of better known artists.

TWO CLERICAL ARTISTS COMPARED: PARKER AND PETIT

Only once does he mention meeting a fellow artist. While staying at Caerynwch (a house 'in a truly splendid situation') near Dolgellau, in August 1846, he walked with 'Mr Meredith Richards above the house, to a place where Mr Burt an artist of Birmingham is painting in oils a torrent scene'.[40] Charles Thomas Burt (1823–1902) was a landscape painter, born in Wolverhampton, but who lived in Birmingham for most of his life; his view of the Mawddach estuary can be seen today in Wolverhampton Art Gallery.

A near contemporary artist with whom Parker had a

'Cnicht'

great deal in common was John Louis Petit (1801–1868). Like Parker he came from a wealthy, landed family; the boys were contemporaries at Eton after which Parker went to Oxford and Petit to Cambridge, and subsequently both took Holy Orders. Parker spent all his life as a clergyman but Petit, after serving as a curate at Lichfield and later Bradfield in Essex, resigned in 1834 to devote himself to writing, painting and lecturing. On leaving Essex he lived for a time at Shifnal in Shropshire, Parker's birthplace.[41]

Both wrote extensively about church architecture. Petit's first book, *Remarks on Church Architecture* (1841), was a two-volume survey of the subject covering all historical periods and styles with numerous illustrations by the author, particularly of Gothic churches in France and Germany. Parallels can be found in Parker's unpublished memoranda which include notes 'On Gothic architecture', 'Observations upon Gothic Tracery', 'Memoranda concerning the French Gothic Churches from notes made in 1827 on returning from Italy', as well as detailed comments on rood screens in many Welsh churches.[42] While for Parker Gothic was the only acceptable style for a church, Petit mounted a campaign against the dominance of Gothic in the nineteenth-century; his reservations about the superiority of the Gothic would have prompted acrimonious conversations with Parker had they met.

Like Parker, Petit was an enthusiastic traveller but his journeys took him to more distant parts of the world – as well as France and Germany, he went to Syria, Greece, Constantinople and North Africa. Everywhere he went, he sketched and painted views and buildings, amassing a collection of some 12–15,000 watercolours, many of which were later used to illustrate his books and lectures. His extraordinarily prolific output is almost matched by Parker. These collections, both now housed at the National Library in Aberystwyth, provide a wonderful archive for the study of buildings and topography.

It is as amateur architects who recorded their buildings in paintings that the two men can best be compared. Parker's work on his churches at Llanmyrewig and Llanyblodwel is discussed in a subsequent chapter; here it is Petit's project at Caerdeon that is considered. When designing the chapel, Petit was responding to a commission from his brother-in-law, William Edward Jelf, a notable classical scholar who was a don at Christ Church, Oxford, from 1836 to 1849. In 1850, Jelf built Caerdeon Hall near Barmouth ,where he tutored undergraduates in Classics. In a predominantly Welsh-speaking area, Jelf wanted to hold services in English, so he asked Petit to build a chapel on the estate. This was completed in 1862 and Jelf fought a court case to establish his right to hold English services, which he won, and in 1875 the chapel was consecrated and endowed as a district church.

St Philip's, Caerdeon, is now a Grade 1 listed building, appreciated for its striking site above the Barmouth estuary, the combination of southern European architectural influences and the use of local materials. However, it was not always so well regarded. The year after its completion, *The Ecclesiologist* thought it 'something between a large lodge gate and a lady's rustic dairy'.[43] The *Buildings of Wales* entry is more generous – the church 'suggests a monastery or a small farmhouse in Italy'.[44] Undoubtedly, Parker would have been even more critical.

Petit's watercolours vividly demonstrate both the dramatic impact of the church and how it complements its surroundings. By comparison, Parker's paintings of churches show clearly that he was much more concerned to record accurately – often in great detail – the architectural features of the buildings, including their furnishings; Petit places his church firmly in a landscape rendered in bolder, more impressionistic, style than Parker.

It is a remarkable coincidence that two men from such similar backgrounds have left architectural memorials as provocative and diverse as the campanile at Llanmyrewig, the tower at Llanyblodwel and the chapel at Caerdeon.

John Louis Petit, *Caerdeon church Feb 10th 1862*

John Louis Petit, *Caerdeon church Feb 11th 1862*

PARKER AND THE GOTHIC IN MANUSCRIPTS AND INSCRIPTIONS

Parker's interest in medieval architecture and history prompted an enthusiasm for Gothic lettering and calligraphy. His drawing volumes include many examples of Gothic script copied from medieval manuscripts and still more are his own attempts at imitating the style. A visit to Peniarth gave Parker the opportunity to look at the famous collection of manuscripts originally assembled by Robert Vaughan of Hengwrt. He copied the decoration from 'a Gothic Missal'. Parker also collected inscriptions from churches; the example from Newtown's old St Mary's is interesting as the church was abandoned in the middle of the nineteenth-century, when it was replaced by the new St David's.

In 1836, he visited the Bodleian Library at Oxford and made copies of some illustrations from the *Romance of Alexander*, recently described by Bodley's Librarian as 'the most sumptuously illuminated manuscript the Bodleian owns'.[45] This appealed strongly to Parker's romantic view of medieval history, and his drawings show tents decorated in blue and red. Next to one of these attractive pavilions stands a regal figure holding a halberd. Parker's annotations describe the artwork on the page: 'instead of sky there is a ground of gold foliage pattern on red forming a rich diaper', while the margin has 'oak leaf in [a] running border'. These are just the sort of decorative details that Parker loved to draw in his notebooks alongside the Gothic script he practised.

Twenty years later, the same manuscript inspired another enthusiast of medieval art and tales of chivalry, who became much better known than Parker. William Morris, while an undergraduate at Exeter College, was given permission to view the manuscript. Soon afterwards, Morris and other Pre-Raphaelites decorated the library of the Oxford Union with Arthurian scenes influenced by the *Romance*.

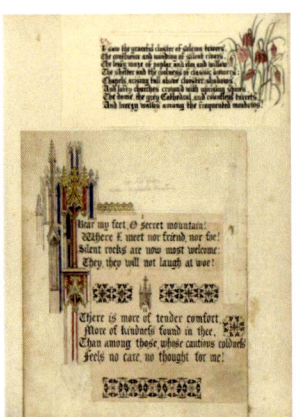

Examples of calligraphy and illumination

Part of psalm 110 in Latin in the style of an illuminated manuscript

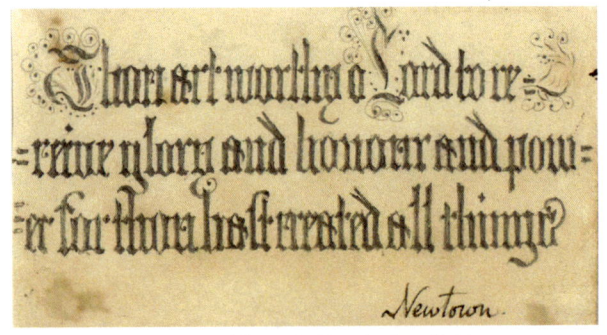

Inscription copied from St Mary's church, Newtown

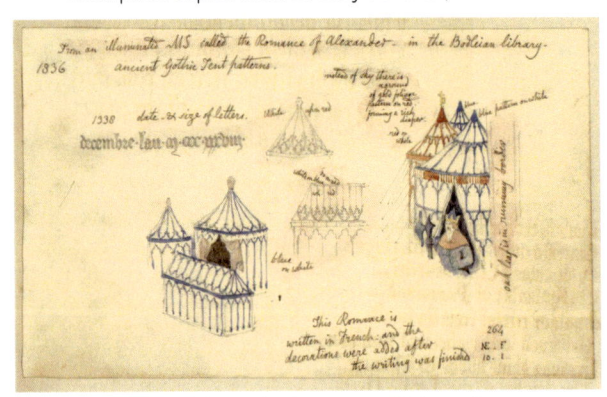

Copied from the *Romance of Alexander* at the Bodleian Library, Oxford

31 Freeman, *op. cit.* for further information about portraits of the Ladies.

32 For the history of the house, see Melvin Humphreys, *Garth: Estate, Architecture and Family,* privately published, 2020.

33 Alex Taylor at Eton kindly provided information about Samuel Evans.

34 The National Portrait Gallery website, *British Artists' Suppliers, 1650–1950.*

35 Simon Cobb, *John Boydell and the depiction of Welsh scenery in reproductive prints, 1750–1850,* The National Library of Wales Journal, Volume XXXVII, No. 4, 2017, p.534.

36 Peter Lord, *The Visual Culture of Wales: Imaging the Nation,* University of Wales Press, 2000, 153. Chapters 4 and 5, Ancient Britain and the Idea of Landscape, explain the development of landscape painting in Wales, with beautifully reproduced examples of artists' works.

37 The National Library has a collection of over 150 of Smith's paintings, all of which have been digitised and can be viewed online.

38 For a discussion of the ways artists have depicted Snowdonia see Peter Bishop, *The Mountains of Snowdonia in Art: The Visualisation of Mountain Scenery from the mid-Eighteenth Century to the Present Day* Gwasg Carreg Gwalch, 2015.

The same author's article *Thomas Pennant (1726–98), The Journey to Snowdon and its influence on artists visiting Wales,* The British Art Journal, Volume XIX, No. 3 2018/2019, pp.87–95, identifies many artists who followed Pennant's examples.

39 Personal communication to the author 27th November 2021.

40 For Caerynwch, see Richard Haslam, Julian Orbach and Adam Voelcker, *op. cit.,* 563. The Meredith Richards who Parker mentions was the son of the owner Richard Richards (1786–1860) MP for Merioneth between 1836 and 1852.

41 Philip Mondiano, 'The Revd J L Petit (1801–1868) and the beauty of churches', *The British Art Journal,* vol. 18 (2) 2017, 40–49; see also the Rev. J. L. Petit society's website (revpetit.com). The National Library has two boxes of Petit's watercolours (John Louis Petit, Original Drawings, Solander Bocs 1 + 2), the first containing fifteen views of the church at Caerdeon, the second a variety of Welsh subjects, including Caernarfon castle, Penmon Priory and Devil's Bridge. In 2020, the NLW received the Ian Cooke collection of thousands of Petit's works, which have yet to be catalogued.

For a fuller discussion of Petit's significance see Philip Modiano, *J.L. Petit: Britain's Lost Pre-Impressionist,* RPS Publications, 2022

42 NLW MS 19382E, *passim.*

43 Rachel Morley, 'St Philip's Chapel, Caerdeon', in *The Building Conservation Directory: Special Report on Historic Churches,* 27th Annual Edition.

44 Richard Haslam, Julian Orbach and Adam Voelcker, *op. cit,* 567.

45 Richard Ovenden, *Burning the Books,* John Murray, 2020, 68.

Chapter Nine
Parker and the buildings of North Wales

'Tan y Bwlch'

Parker's sketches and paintings include studies of mountains, rocks and waterfalls alongside plants and flowers, but these are outnumbered by drawings of buildings. As well as recording existing buildings, he drew hundreds of designs for churches and church furnishings – from pulpits to crucifixes – all in Gothic style. Parker was more than a keen amateur, his notes and drawings of churches, in particular of screens and fonts, are invaluable to historians because he visited churches before drastic restorations altered their appearance and often swept away examples of the medieval woodwork which he revered.

When Parker first came to North Wales many of the historic buildings, now frequented by thousands of visitors, were in a parlous state; most were in private hands and access was not always willingly granted nor were the owners necessarily concerned about their preservation. Parker's comments and descriptions anticipate the upsurge of interest in their preservation, initiated by the Cambrian Archaeological Association and county historical societies, which eventually resulted in measures to protect them. In the first volume of *Archaeologia Cambrensis* in 1846, the editors expressed the hope 'that by describing and illustrating the antiquities of our native land we shall meet with the lasting support and sympathy of all'. Under the leadership of Harry Longueville Jones, the journal of the Association became a forum for discussion of how best to preserve and protect the historic monuments of Wales. These aims met with Parker's enthusiastic approval; he spent much of his life doing exactly what this manifesto proposed. He was an early member of the Association and, in 1847, was appointed the Local Secretary for Shropshire. Although he appears not to have contributed to the journal, his work is acknowledged in articles published in the last century on Strata Florida and Abbey Cwm-hir and, more particularly, in the series of papers by Crossley and Ridgway on the screens and lofts of Wales.

'Valle Crucis Abbey near Llangollen'

CHURCHES AND THEIR FURNISHINGS

In *The Passengers*, Parker made a clear distinction between his admiration for Gothic architecture and his distaste for 'monkish errors, and the corruptions of Roman Catholic idolatry' practised in medieval churches and monasteries. By comparison with the great cathedrals and impressive parish churches he described on his tour to Winchester, Salisbury and Bristol in 1838, North Wales could offer few such impressive buildings.

He was disappointed that, 'The North welch abbies [*sic*] with the exception of Basingwerk and Vale crucis have suffered more than those of England.' Valle Crucis, near Llangollen, was on his route to Snowdonia and Parker visited it many times and made sketches of the ruins and of architectural details. On one occasion in September 1832, he 'had a dispute with the tenant of the farmhouse who being deprived of the patronage of the abbey, wishes to annoy visitors, by preventing their examination of her premises, which composed the ancient Refectory – measured various parts for an hour, and went through the church ruins'. In *The Passengers*, he made the odd claim that, 'It was a Cistercian Abbey, that is to say, it consisted of Monks as well as Nuns.' While there had been some 'double monasteries' which accommodated religious of both sexes in Anglo-Saxon England and later in the twelfth-century, the Cistercians never permitted such mixing.

In August 1828, he went to the site of Maenan (Llanrwst) Abbey. 'I expected to recognize in the owner of Llanrwst abbey a gentleman who had kindly taken a small valise of mine in his gig from Waterloo Bridge [the bridge in Betws-y-coed, dated 1815] to Llanrwst and who asked me to call on him any day before I left the country. But Mr Lyas the present owner of Llanrwst abbey was not this person, and though I believe my acquaintance was staying at the house he was not at home and I did not enter into an explanation but confined myself to architectural enquiries.' Lyas showed him the abbey site, 'no part of which can at present be traced above ground, one small gothic arch in the cellar is the only visible proof of its existence'. Parker was told that 'The foundations of the church were discovered some years ago by Lord Newborough then … the owner of the property, but no plan was taken.'

The cathedral at Bangor 'is not handsome'; he

'Early English basement, West end of Abbey Crucis discovered by excavation 1851'

regretted that 'The tower is exceedingly mean and the total absence of pinnacles in the body of the church gives it a low appearance.' However, his comments need to be treated with caution as he was uncharacteristically inaccurate in his account of the history of the building; he claimed 'Bishop Skeffington has the credit of having built this cathedral in 1582.' In fact, Skevington (the more usual spelling) died in 1533 and was responsible for the tower.

One feature of some Welsh churches he deplored were the ceilings which had been inserted in the previous hundred years to make them less cold and draughty. At Bangor, the nave plaster ceiling was 'not of good character or design, and I should almost prefer the timber roof to the bad gothic which now conceals it'. The church at Llanerfyl in north Montgomeryshire had 'a very bad modern ceiling [which] destroys the internal effect of this nice handsome church'. One of the benefits of the restorations which affected Welsh churches so dramatically – in and after Parker's lifetime – was the removal of such ceilings, which exposed fine, early timber roofs. (The introduction of more efficient heating systems encouraged this change.) But some restorations obliterated the furnishings of country churches, as was the case at Garthbeibio, close to Llanerfyl. Parker's drawing of 1846 shows an impressive barrel roof with fine bosses over the chancel, box pews and a three-decker pulpit, all swept away in the restoration of 1862.

Parker was less interested in funerary monuments than in screens and fonts but on his 1833 tour he found examples which commemorated famous people and stirring events in Welsh history. On Tuesday 2 July, he crossed from Bangor to Anglesey by the Garth Point ferry, walked the mile to Beaumaris and, after dinner at the Bulkeley Arms, he 'went in search of Queen Joan's monument'. In 1205, Joan, or Siwan, the illegitimate daughter of King John, married Llywelyn ap Iorwerth (the Great) and henceforth, until her death in 1237, she played an important part in Llywelyn's government, particularly in his diplomacy with England. Joan was buried at Llan-faes, where Llywelyn founded the Franciscan friary in her memory. At the dissolution of the friary in 1537, her sarcophagus was, in Parker's words, 'removed from Llanfaes Priory [and] was used for some time as a watering trough'. This is just one example of the grievous loss of many fine monuments resulting from the dissolution of the monasteries, which were the

'Montgomeryshire Garthbibio [sic] Church 1845'

favoured burial sites of many royal and noble families. Parker only found the stone coffin – after 'a passing stranger set me right' – in a 'modern Gothic building which a few years ago sheltered the Sarcophagus, lying in fragments on the ground, while a couple of rustic arches in rough branchwork were being put up instead of it'. An inscription recorded the removal of the coffin to this place of safety by Lord Bulkeley in 1802. Subsequently, it was placed in the parish church of Beaumaris where it can be seen today. However, recent scholarship has cast doubt on this being Joan's monument and it is more likely to commemorate Eleanor de Montfort.[46]

Llandygai monument to Archbishop Williams, with the permission of RCAHMW

The church at Llandygái near Penrhyn castle was unprepossessing: 'The square central tower, slated on the sides, does not look well.' However, Parker was more enthusiastic about 'the three monuments of interest and importance belonging to the Penrhyn family'. But the memorial to John Williams, Archbishop of York under Charles I, prompted an unusual anti-Welsh comment from Parker: 'in those unhappy times, the Cambrian failing, a sacrifice of principle to personal feeling induced him to desert the royalist side at the siege of Conway.' (In 1642 Williams had been responsible for fortifying and holding Conwy castle as a Royalist stronghold but he was ejected in 1645 by a fellow Royalist and in 1646, believing the King's cause to be lost, he joined the parliamentarians in storming the castle.) The style of the monument – typical of the mid-seventeenth-century – with an open pediment supported on Corinthian columns, Parker considered to be 'in the second rate Roman style of that period'. He suggested that, 'Open ironwork arranged in some sort of curve so as to give the semblance of an arch [and] Gothic tracery would have been beautiful here, but the Roman style having been adopted, that is now out of the question.'

If monuments of high quality were rare, many churches had fine woodwork. Welsh churches still have impressive fifteenth-century oak roofs, but the real gems, particularly for Parker, were the wooden screens which divided the chancel from the nave. The purpose of the screen was originally to distinguish the priest's part of the church from the congregation's in the nave. Above the screen there was a rood or cross – hence the term rood screen – and other religious images which were decorated on important religious festivals. The rood loft was approached by a staircase usually hollowed out of the chancel arch. The woodwork of the screen was decorated with panels of geometric designs and carvings of fruit, vine leaves and sometimes mythical beasts. The quality of the carving was – and still is – of breathtaking skill and sophistication. Much of the woodwork was originally painted, in reds and blues and gilded in places.

By Parker's time, screens had suffered many vicissitudes. Protestant reformers objected to what they considered idolatrous worship of the images above the screen and most were taken down in the mid-sixteenth-century; in some cases, the destruction of the screen itself followed. In subsequent centuries, many rural churches fell into disrepair and screens suffered dilapidation if not worse. The great tide of church restoration in the nineteenth-century coincided with new ideas about the organisation of church interiors – a clear view of the altar from the nave was seen as desirable – and these two factors also resulted in the loss of some medieval screens.

Parker's tour journals before 1828 include only one reference to a screen; on 10 September 1821, while staying at Bodowen, he noted 'the ruins of a screen' in the church at Llanaber. Seven years later, he began a series of drawings of the fine screen in St Mary's Church, Newtown, and in the same year he visited for the first time the tiny church at Llananno in Radnorshire when he was returning home from an expedition to Abbey Cwm-hir. He was unable to obtain the key, so he had to peer through the windows and 'saw a superb chancel screen in high preservation which I must make a point of examining on my return'. Subsequent visits confirmed his first impressions and he later wrote that the Llananno screen was 'a specimen of perfection in ornamental carpentry that no other age or style can approach or equal'.

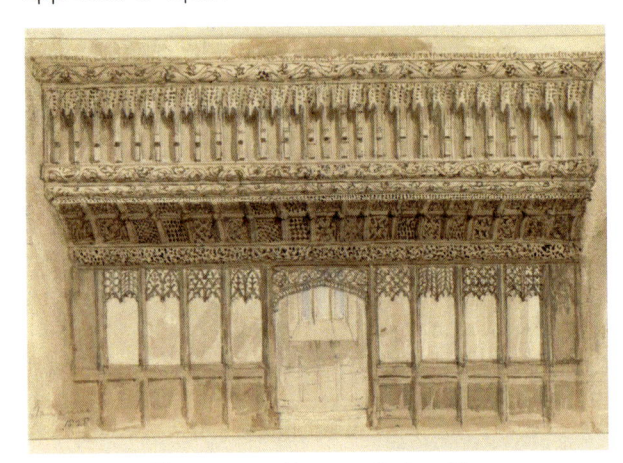

The screen at Llananno, Radnorshire

His appreciation of the craftsmanship of these late medieval screens, allied to his skill as a draughtsman, has led to Parker being revered by later scholars. In 1943, Fred H. Crossley published the first in a series of articles (in *Archaeologia Cambrensis*) on the 'screens, lofts and stalls of Wales and Monmouthshire'. By 1946, he had covered North Wales and, from 1947, in collaboration with Maurice H. Ridgway, the series was extended to include South Wales. The result is a comprehensive guide with detailed descriptions and analysis of all such features in Welsh churches. In the introduction to the first article, Crossley included a dedication: 'To the Gracious Memory of THE REV. JOHN PARKER, admirable artist and diligent antiquary, whose labours have given to us a knowledge of the work of many mediaeval craftsmen now destroyed by the malice of time and restorers.' Such a generous tribute is a reminder that Parker was much more than a dilettante tourist and that the archive of his works in words and pictures is of enduring worth to everyone interested in the history of Wales.

The two tours he made to North Wales in 1828 and 1829 were chiefly to view fine examples of screens. The first, which he described rather grandly as 'a Gothic tour of Carnarvonshire', actually only involved visits to Llanrwst (in Denbighshire) and Conwy, but in both places he found screens to delight him. Of Llanrwst church, he repeated a phrase he used in *The Passengers*: it 'has no pretensions to grandeur or elegance. Like most of the Welch [sic] Churches it appears to be the chief barn of the neighbourhood.' Today, most visitors to the church are attracted by the Gwydir Chapel and its monuments, of which Parker was very dismissive. He writes, '[It] is rather celebrated [but] is a small building, of bad gothic, hardly worth notice'; the unusual funerary monuments inside he thought 'altho somewhat costly, are below mediocrity when considered as works of art'. ... 'The church however contains a superb chancel screen, removed from the Abbey of Maenan about three miles lower down the Conway river ... There is a gallery above and the whole screen has apparently been more valued than its contemporaries in other places.' In fact, the screen did not come from the abbey; he made a similar misleading claim for the screen at Newtown, which he described as originating from Abbey Cwm-hir.

Parker measured the screen and made detailed drawings of the carvings; he considered that 'The perpendicular part ... has a close resemblance to those of Radnorshire and the Newtown neighbourhood but the lower part is totally different and is altogether the finest work of its kind that can be met with.' Crossley's account of the screen includes copies of Parker's illustrations ('beautifully drawn') and he concurs with Parker in recognising the mixture of English and Welsh elements in the construction and decoration of the screen.

One of Parker's qualities as a writer on architecture is his wide knowledge of buildings and their furnishings, in Britain and beyond. He had an enviable memory which prompted comparisons, as in this case, with 'some woodwork at the east end of the north aisle of St Alban's, and two very fine ones in the aisle of Ludlow church, but none are so tastefully disposed as this of Llanrwst'. He also remarked on the 'the double vine pattern [on the screen] resembling the magnificent one at Newtown'. On its east side, the screen was decorated with 'mullion patterns like those of Llanwnog'. The next day, his inspection of the screen was delayed because Bishop Luxmoore – his bishop – arrived to conduct a confirmation service; to Parker's amazement, he 'confirmed 360 without any signs of exhaustion'. After some conversation with his Lordship, Parker resumed his examination of the screen and was pleased to find two pieces of woodwork underneath the reading desk which he took back to the inn where he was staying 'to copy at my leisure'.

He decided to keep these two fragments as 'It cannot be generally known or acknowledged that altho ancient works of gothic art should ever be held sacred from the hands of covetous curiosity, still when separate fragments of them are discovered by those who understand their value, no impediment should be thrown in the way of their obtaining them.' This acquisitive attitude was typical of the antiquarians of the period, some of whom built up remarkable collections of very diverse

Llanrwst details of the screen

items. (Parker had earlier referred to his possession of part of the screen from Llanegryn church.) However, when he informed the parish clerk of his intention, he was told that the churchwarden would have to be consulted; that led to a conversation with the curate, who told Parker that the rector (unsurprisingly, his uncle) had said no part of the screen was to be removed. Parker respected his fellow cleric's authority and returned the pieces to the church. But in his journal he voiced his fears for their future: 'If the Rector is so concerned about the screen why is it in its present parlous state? One of the main beams on the western side has been half cut through to make way for a door.'

The next day, 'Friday 22nd Set off in a one horse 'car' and a boy to drive to Conway.' He found another impressive screen which, although 'in a ruinous condition ... is a most rich example of the fan groining in wood and it compares with that in stone at King's Cambridge, Westminster abbey and St George's chapel Windsor'. He was struck particularly by 'the oak border' with its great variety of subjects: 'birds, beasts, fishes and grapes with the Prince of Wales plume of Ostrich feathers'. Parker was one of the first writers to draw attention to the high quality of Welsh craftsmanship, which had been ignored, or subject to what Rosemary Sweet refers to as 'assumptions about English superiority and dominance within the British Isles'.[47] In 1830, Parker wrote 'A small treatise upon Welsh Gothic ... in north Wales churches' in which he drew attention to the preservation of remarkable screens in churches 'conspicuous for no other beauties, and utterly devoid of exterior grandeur, [it] is indeed a singular accident in the history of Gothic art. England tho' so rich in gothic woodwork, does not I believe, contain any specimens like these.'[48] Unfortunately, Parker's day in Conwy was spoiled by the exorbitant charges at the Castle Hotel, where he 'paid 3s.2d for them looking after the boy and the horse for three hours'.

In 1829, he began his tour later than usual – on 25 September – by the mail coach to Bangor, which he reached at 10.30 p.m. The next day, unsurprisingly, he decided not to take the early coach at 6 a.m. for Pwllheli, but waited for the 9 a.m. service. On this foray into the Llŷn Peninsula, he visited two churches which were far from the barn-like buildings Parker often commented on: Clynnog Fawr, on the north coast, and Llanengan, deep in the quiet countryside between Pwllheli and Aberdaron. Both have impressive early sixteenth-century crenellated towers, spacious naves and aisles lit by large east-facing windows. The reason for this grand architectural display was pilgrimage; both churches benefitted from people making the journey to Aberdaron to brave the dangerous short sea passage to Ynys Enlli (Bardsey Island). The tiny island, reputedly the burial place of 20,000 saints, was 'known as a second Rome on account of so great a concentration of holiness within so small a compass'.[49]

Clynnog Fawr church, photograph National Churches Trust

At Clynnog, Parker stayed at the Newborough Arms (which has since been called the New Inn and the St

'Clynog Vawr Sept. 30 1829'

'A boss on the panelled ceiling of the Nave of Clynog Vawr, Carnarvonshire'

'Llanengan in Lleyn. Details of the screen'

Beuno Inn but is now the Newborough once more) opposite the church. He was not as impressed by the exterior of the church as modern visitors on account of his aversion to the Perpendicular style, which he regarded as a debased form of Gothic. Inside he found a screen similar to that at Llanrwst, but not, he thought, of the same quality.

At Llanengan, the rector, the Reverend W. L. Jones, provided accommodation but his guest was laid low by a bad cold for most of the time. Nonetheless, Parker made drawings of the screen and sketched a view of the church from his sickbed. On his way back to Bangor, he stopped again at Clynnog to complete his examination of the church. As well as the descriptions in his journals and the drawings, Parker also wrote memoranda on the screens at Llanengan and Clynnog and took detailed measurements of those at Conwy and Llanrwst.

After the churches at Clynnog and Llanengan, Parker was very disappointed to make a return visit to Bangor cathedral, where he deplored 'the modern gothic in the choir [which] is of the most odious and vulgar description. It is by far the worst attempt at the style that I ever saw.' Like so many of the churches he described, the cathedral was extensively restored later, in this case by George Gilbert Scott and his son John Oldrid Scott, and the east end that Parker criticised was completely remodelled.

He never tired in his efforts to persuade people of the artistic quality of the woodwork to be found in remote Welsh churches. In July 1838, when he was exploring Winchester cathedral, Parker noted the 'screen work in wood' which partly surrounds Langton's Chantry and the Lady Chapel. 'This woodwork, however, has neither the boldness nor the richness of the Welch [sic] chancel screens; and several of the barnlike churches in the Principality surpass in this respect the sumptuous cathedral of Winchester.'

A drawing Parker made in 1849 of the interior of St Mary's church, Conwy, shows the nave from the west end and prominent in the foreground is the elaborately carved fifteenth-century font.

'Painting the font at Llanmerewic, August 22, 1838'

Although by their very size and weight fonts were less likely to be discarded or damaged than screens, a considerable number were thrown out during Victorian restorations. In his church at Llanmyrewig, Parker rescued the medieval font which had been used 'for farm purposes'. On 22 August 1838, Parker painted a charming picture of a young man decorating the new, replacement font; the old, damaged one he placed in the chancel with an inscription explaining its provenance. After screens, fonts became Parker's next focus of interest in churches. In one of his drawing volumes, he included sketches of forty-two examples, most from Wales and a few from border counties. In addition there are brief notes on the style of fifty-seven fonts, he also attached nineteen designs of his own. Parker's skill as a draughtsman is evident in his meticulous attention to the decorative details. Of the fonts in Snowdonia only one is no longer in situ, the undecorated simple bowl at Llandderfel near Bala was replaced by a sandstone font in 1870.

THE EDWARDIAN CASTLES

Parker thought the great castles built by Edward I at Conwy, Caernarfon and Beaumaris 'finer than any to be found on the Continent ... such as the meagre and domestic looking castle of Chillon ... [which] are wondered at and eulogized whereas the north Wales castles are visited by few tourists'. Chillon on Lake Geneva attracted famous tourists such as Victor Hugo, Alexandre Dumas and Lord Byron, who lauded the castle as the most romantic medieval fortress. Parker was unconvinced. In August 1828, he was at Conwy: 'This is the first time I have seen [the castle] since going up the Rhine. How greatly superior these truly romantic towers are to those petty, homely looking ruins that stand within three or four miles of each other on that river!'

While he admired the Edwardian castles, he was concerned that they were not well cared for and his descriptions include comments on the worrying state of the fabric. At Caernarfon in 1820, he feared for the state of the castle, commenting, 'It is just in the same state as it was some years ago, altho' in many parts it seems nodding to its fall.' However, he was impressed by 'the endless galleries, which run all around the outside walls communicating with geometrical staircases, ramparts and halls, yet multiplied, apparently with such lavish extravagance as to give more the idea of a building hewn out of solid rock, than artificially raised by an architect'. Nine years later, he noted that the Eagle Tower was 'injured last year 1828 by lightning – stones thrown out of their places'. It was to Caernarfon that he returned on his last journey in 1860, and the drawings he did on

'Corridor in Carnarvon castle 1832'

'Queen Eleanor's Gateway, Carnarvon Castle'

'Caernarvon June 12 1860'

12 June show he had lost none of his skill and that his interest in the details of medieval architecture was as keen as ever. Because he was such a frequent visitor, he noticed important changes to the fabric of buildings, as in the window tracery at Conwy restored between his visits in 1820 and early 1827. Beaumaris castle he noted, 'altho inferior in size & loftiness to Conway and

Conwy Castle

The chapel at Beaumaris castle

'A ruined window in Conway castle as it appeared in 1820' and 'The same restored'

Carnarvon yet in point of picturesque effect inside it surpasses both.' He was particularly impressed, in October 1829, by the chapel: 'the most elegant early Gothic chapel – the vaulting entire – with a hexagonal termination, an enlargement of the beautiful oriel at Conway'. However 'above this fine specimen of groining I found a garden of potatoes & cabbages! Mr Bulkeley Williams of Barron Hill is the owner of the castle.' Four years later, while staying in Beaumaris, Parker spent hours in the castle chapel, where he 'got a ladder by which I reached the groining ... and measured various parts of it'.

He visited Harlech at least twice, in 1820 and 1823, but has left no drawing of the castle. On the first visit, while he found the castle 'impressive', it was the view of 'the beautiful outlines of the first-rate mountains, Wythva [sic] pre-eminently soaring [above] them', that engaged his attention. On this occasion, when he and his companion, Neave, had luncheon, Parker noted 'a large picture of the meeting at Manchester shewing the arrest of Hunt & with references below in the radical style, in as much as they abounded not only in falsehood, but in bad spelling'. This is a reference to the Peterloo meeting in 1819 which ended in bloodshed when the yeomanry charged into a crowd of peaceful protesters killing eighteen and injuring many more. It is interesting that the scene is displayed in a public room so soon after the event happened. Parker's response to the print is what one would expect from a man of his upbringing and it is one of the very few references in the hundreds of pages of his journals to a contemporary event. His second visit to Harlech in June 1823 prompted a brief, critical comment, 'Sir R. Vaughan's New Inn sadly interferes with the castle.'

GENTRY HOUSES

One advantage Parker enjoyed over some other tourists was his easy access to the houses of the local gentry. In part, this was simply because he himself came from a gentry family, but it was made easier in Merionethshire through his uncle's friendships with local notables. He stayed at Bodowen in September 1821 and 'after church rode to Corsygedol an old family mansion of Sir Thomas Mostyn's about 4 miles away'. He described the house thus: 'In all its parts and colours and arrangements [it is] opposite to everything like modern convenience.' The fenestration was a mixture of 'windows with stone mullions, others with modern sashes'. They were let into the house by Miss Williams, the daughter of Sir Thomas's agent: 'The inside of Corsygedol is like the outside, straggling, odd and inconvenient. Lots of family portraits in the large low drawing room; the every corner of the stairs surmounted by a ramping lion and a shield, there are old velvet state beds.' Three days later, he went with his uncle to Nannau, where they met Sir Robert Vaughan, who gave them luncheon. While he thought the scenery between Bodowen and Dolgellau was 'beyond all description superb', Nannau he found 'not handsome but convenient and pleasing … three stories [sic], small porch in front; the entrance room between the dining and breakfast rooms is a small aviary. The garden some distance from the house.'

The owners of such grand houses incurred responsibilities and obligations; in this matter, Parker was surely influenced by the example of his father, who took a keen, practical interest in the well-being of his local community. He reported that Sir Robert Vaughan 'is always employing people on cottages, lodges, roads, plantations and all things of that kind flourish around him and his constant residence at Nannau must greatly increase the comforts of the poor. For five years past he has afforded constant employment to twenty five masons.' Two years later, in 1823, he expressed his disappointment that the same could not be said of the absentee squire of Plas Tan y Bwlch, at Maentwrog. Parker met the vicar of the neighbouring parish of Llandecwyn, who 'informed me that Mr Oakley [the family name is usually spelled Oakeley, they were the owners of the Blaenau Ffestiniog slate quarries] had gone to the neighbourhood of London in order to live cheaply as he found this country too expensive. Mr Oakley however married a Bath wife. He is said to be of studious habits, reserved and fonder of books than of society. The man for such a neighbourhood as this would be of an active public and enterprising character, one that should superintend these infamous roads and introduce the civilization of England among his Welch tenantry.'

He visited Peniarth, the home of William Watkin Edward Wynne, the great antiquarian, whom Parker would also have known through the Cambrian Archaeological Association. The church at Llanegryn where the Wynnes were buried was familiar to Parker on account of its splendid rood screen. In fact, 'by a singular accident some fragments of it were given to me several years ago after being carried away to a distance, and I have promised Wynne of Peniarth whenever he begins to restore this screen that I will gladly restore them.'

One of Wales's oldest houses, Gwydir, disappointed Parker. He first saw it in 1820, when he noted: 'On to Llanrwst and Gwydir house, a singular specimen of grey antiquity and obsolete architecture.' Six years later, he took a closer look and found the house 'a fragment of what it was full of the traces of past neglect, and later more cautious repairs but yet rather clumsy'. But he 'found also an excellent gothic pattern of circular quatrefoils with very masterly foliations between them. This was at the top of that barbarous yet handsome escutcheon which has figures of Julius and Augustus as supporters and occupies all the space over the chimney in the room on the ground floor.' Parker is here describing one of the grand chimney pieces which the present owners, Peter Welford and Judy Corbett, have been trying to locate after it was sold with many other items to William Randolph Hearst in 1921. Parker's third reference to the house is more encouraging; in 1828, he found that the owners 'are slowly repairing it in a corresponding style to the ancient work'.

Gwydir castle, overmantel, by permission of Judy Corbett and Peter Welford

'Rhiwedog nr Bala J Parker Sept 4 1846'

In 1846, near Bala, he came to an old house whose architecture and legendary place in Welsh history appealed to his antiquarian interests. 'Friday Septr 4 Drove to Rhiwedog [sic] an old mansion partly built in 1664, other portions earlier and some later – much out of repair ... only half inhabited by the tenant farmer who lives in it. Here in the 6th century stood the palace of Llywarch Hen the warrior, prince & Bard, whose twenty four sons fell in battle and their father outlived them. The last of the sons fell in an engagement with the Saxons in 580 on this ground which is therefore called Rhiwaelog the bloody bank. This old house at present belongs to Mr Price of Rhiwlas. A gatehouse on the north side of the mansion leads to a small court, a datestone 1664 with initials I LL S; stone mullioned windows.' These old mansions had very thick stone walls but the lack of mortar and the use of wooden mullions in larger windows meant that lintels frequently cracked and 'their chimnies [sic] are seldom upright'.

On his 'Sketching Tour of North Wales' in 1840, Parker made a detour on his way to Machynlleth and 'left the turnpike at the New Inn and reached the old mansion of Aberlleveny [Aberllefenni] the eastern wing

Aberllefenni, from the collection of Tom Lloyd

Greenfields later The Plas, Machynlleth

may be of gothic date ... the rest modernized ... the old windows have been cut out in order to introduce two rows of sash windows without any mouldings'. The wing he mentions was demolished in the twentieth-century. In Machynlleth, he visited the most recently built of the large houses of the area, Greenfields (later Y Plas). The core of the building is an eighteenth-century house, but it was refronted in the 1830s and, as Parker comments, work was still continuing in 1840. 'May 30 after breakfast at the Wynnstay Arms, to the church to draw the font; then drove to the north lodge of Greenfields ... this entrance is of castle Gothic and is not completed. It is well designed, Sir John & Lady Edwards not at home, left a card; the house is modern, cream-coloured with an eastern portico; the neighbouring town very skilfully concealed from the house and grounds.' Here at Machynlleth, Parker found a squire fulfilling those duties incumbent on the gentry, acting as a colonel in the militia, as High Sheriff and, in the 1830s, as the Member of Parliament for the Montgomeryshire boroughs. He also had the good sense to flank the gates leading to his house with lodges in Gothic style.

CONTEMPORARY BUILDINGS

The early nineteenth-century was a period of enormous change, particularly in transport. The Industrial Revolution involved the movement of large amounts of heavy materials such as coal, iron, slate and bricks; roads had to be improved, new canals were dug and, in the 1830s, railways began to link the larger cities. On his journeys from Sweeney to North Wales, Parker saw impressive examples of the work of Thomas Telford. Shortly after leaving Oswestry, coach passengers passed close to one of the marvels of the age – the Pontcysyllte aqueduct which carried the Ellesmere canal over the River Dee. In *The Passengers*, Clanvoy explains to his companions, 'Below the level of the road, and at some distance off, you see the Aqueduct of Pont Cysyllty, which I do not ask you to admire from here; but, if you were to go over it and under it, you would find it greatly superior to that of Chirk. It is considered to be some of the finest masonry in the kingdom. The pillars are of stone, from the neighbouring quarries of Ruabon; but the whole trough of the canal and the towing-path is of iron.' Completed in 1805, it soon became one of the great sights of the age and visitors marvelled at the 'stream in the sky'.[50]

The whole route of the 'Irish Road', from Shrewsbury

'Pontcysyllte aqueduct April May 1811'

to Holyhead, was surveyed and improved by Telford between 1815 and 1826. This involved major reconstruction of the road through the mountains and the building of new bridges at Betws-y-coed, Conwy and, most dramatically, across the Menai Strait. The building of the suspension bridge across the River Conwy, so close to the medieval castle, was a major challenge, but Parker was impressed by the result. 'I was greatly pleased with the new suspension bridge, the stone of which is much too white at present but adjoining as it does to the castle and corresponding with it in style. I never saw so fine an instance of the genius of ancient art influencing modern science.'

The suspension bridge spanning the Menai Strait, Telford's engineering masterpiece, prompted ambivalent responses from Parker. 'An electric shock of wonder is felt by every one when first passing over the Menai Bridge' and he was excited by the sight of 'a large vessel in full sail under it; a loaded coach may now drive over the main top gallant of a British frigate.' However his praise was qualified: 'the science of the construction may continue to delight the mechanic, but it is no longer acknowledged as a fine work of art.' He regretted Telford's use of 'the Roman style' for the arches on the towers, where he felt – unsurprisingly – 'Gothic tracery would have been beautiful here'. He made similar remarks about the Crystal Palace when he visited the Great Exhibition in 1851. 'Had Mr Paxton been an architect as well as an engineer, this building would possibly have been so constructed as to satisfy some requirement of style and might have become capable of a prolonged existence. But, as it is, there is, I cannot help saying a mixture of Chinese and cockney character in the general effect of it.' (For Parker, 'cockney' character' was a term of deep disdain.)

The Menai Bridge, engraving by W. Crane, Chester, c. 1860

Close to the Menai Bridge, on the site of an earlier house, Lord Penrhyn was building one of the largest mansions in Britain, as befitted a fabulously wealthy landowner, whose fortune was based on slavery and slate quarries. Penrhyn Castle is built in a Norman revival style and on a scale which matches the mightiest Edwardian castles. Visits to country houses were popular excursions for travellers in the eighteenth and nineteenth centuries and, in June 1833, Parker obtained a ticket for entry to Penrhyn, from the landlady of the inn at Capel Curig, who 'had three of these to dispose of every week and all who can go take these opportunities'. He noted, 'Penrhyn

The Marquis of Anglesey's column

castle is now finished as to general outline, and has become a grey colour, so that it looks as old as Conway or Carnarvon.' Parker was impressed – as modern visitors are – by the sheer scale of Penrhyn; the great hall 'will be a most enormous collection of arcades and heavy Norman groining' and the whole building 'when complete will exhibit a wonderful specimen of adherence to style'. The furniture is Norman 'even to a painful exactness'. But, of course, he had reservations: 'that style, not being the best' because 'I perceive that the Norman style pleases most when it approaches the higher elegance of the pure Gothic.' Port Lodge nearby, built before the castle, was in Parker's view 'a very fine specimen of Norman style'. The Gwynedd *Pevsner* is rather dismissive, describing the Lodge as 'a stylistically indecisive, medievalizing composition', which is, no doubt, why it appealed to Parker.[51]

On the opposite side of the Strait from Penrhyn was another addition to the landscape, which Parker first noted in 1820. This was the Anglesey Column, erected in 1816–17 by public subscription in honour of the Marquess of Anglesey, Wellington's second-in-command at Waterloo. 'How the soul glories in whatsoever may record the actions of Waterloo, so rich in proofs of courage, discipline, fortitude and humanity; in their actual grandeur so overpowering to the feelings of an Englishman; in their consequences, of such immense importance, as to deserve being remembered to the latest ages.' Seven years later, Parker visited the battlefield and thought, rather bathetically, 'The plains of Waterloo and the surrounding country look more like some parts of Oxfordshire than any other places that I can remember.' He walked to 'Château Goumont [Hougoumont] where the conflict was hottest, and saw the ruins of the mansion', of which he made a sketch.

In Dolgellau, Parker was critical of the 'new Town Hall erecting here' (he saw it in 1823, the building was completed in 1825) from a design of Mr Haycock of Shrewsbury. Its Palladian style did not please Parker – 'it is in itself ugly, having too high a pitch on the roofs' – but he admitted 'Any building whatever, if it be carefully and neatly built has a good effect in this rugged scenery.'

'The ruins of Chateaugoumont at Waterloo, 11 June 1827'

'Dolgelly and Cader Idris'

102

[46] Madeleine Gray, 'Four weddings, three funerals and a historic detective puzzle: a cautionary tale', *Transactions of the Anglesey Antiquarian Society and Field Club* 2014, 31–46.

[47] Sweet, *op. cit.*, 267

[48] *NLW MS 19382E, 'A small treatise upon Welsh Gothic ... in north Wales churches' 1830* (number 46 in Michael Freeman's index).

[49] Glanmor Williams, *The Welsh Church: From Conquest to Reformation* University of Wales Press 1976, 496.

[50] For the history of the aqueduct see *Pontcysyllte Aqueduct and Canal: Nomination as a World Heritage Site 2008.*

[51] Richard Haslam, Julian Orbach and Adam Voelcker, *op. cit.*, 404.

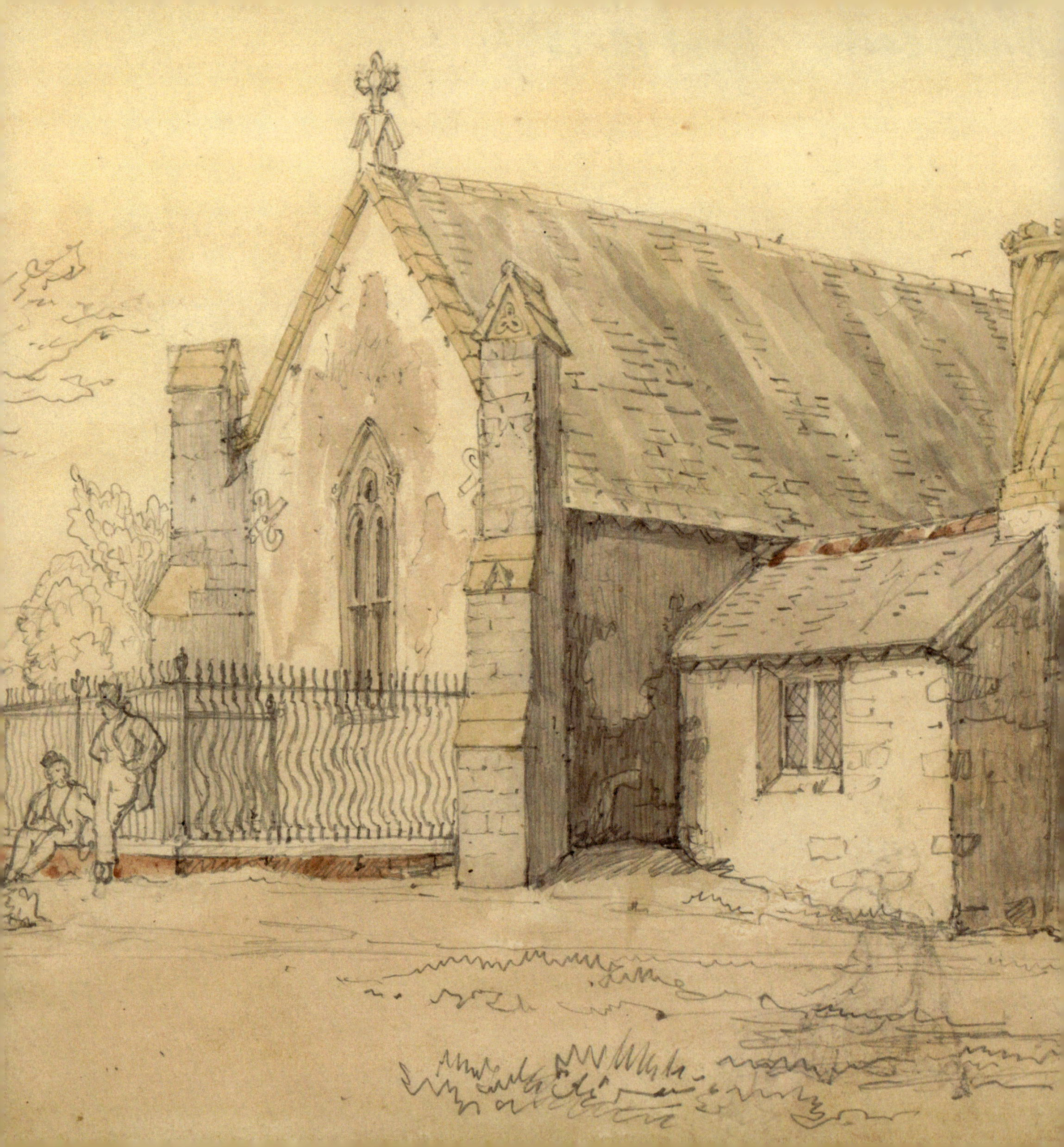

Chapter Ten
Parker the architect and builder

'Llanmarewic from the N.E. April 18 1837'

In many respects, John Parker's interests and attitudes were typical of an educated man of independent means. His passion for the mountains and torrents of North Wales marks him as a Romantic, while his enthusiasm for churches, their architecture and furnishings, places him among the antiquarians whose influence was rapidly gaining ground. He was also one of a small number of Victorian clergymen able to translate his architectural enthusiasm into practice when he undertook the transformation of the two churches in his care.

The confluence of Romanticism and antiquarianism produced a revolution, not only in the way that the countryside and buildings were seen, but also by introducing new attitudes towards the past. The Middle Ages, for so long seen as a period of ignorance and stagnation, were being reinterpreted under the influence of antiquarians and writers, especially Sir Walter Scott. The architecture of the medieval period, labelled Gothic — implying uncivilised — was being rescued from the disdain of the Enlightenment and being studied with fresh eyes.[52] Parker's drawing volumes testify to his passion for Gothic architecture, with their hundreds of sketches of medieval features, including window tracery, corbels, bosses, capitals and ornamental crosses. In addition, there are drawings of churches which he would have liked to build and wonderfully complex designs for fonts and pulpits which remained unrealised.

Parker's obituary in the *Gentleman's Magazine* paid tribute to the part he played in the rehabilitation of Gothic architecture.[53] 'Born, as he was, at a period when architecture had reached its lowest state of degradation, when church architecture was unknown, and churches were uncared for, – devoted from very early years to the study of that art in which not less as a craftsman than as a draughtsman he was peculiarly skilled, – an intimate and friend of earnest-minded Britton, he formed one of that scattered few who sought by intense study of the originals to regain the long-lost principles of Gothic art; and he lived to see those principles acknowledged and firmly established in the ecclesiastical architecture of this country.' While the obituarist exaggerated, with pardonable generosity, the gravity of the state of church architecture in 1800, and Parker's role in its rescue, it is significant that a contemporary viewed him as an influential figure despite the fact that he had published nothing except *The Passengers*. That Parker is described as a friend of Britton is also noteworthy. John Britton (1771–1857) was a self-taught antiquarian, topographer, editor and publisher of extraordinary ambition and energy. 'His influence on the development of the Gothic revival ranks with that of A.W. Pugin and John Ruskin.'[54] It is therefore no surprise to learn that Parker was a friend of such a passionate recorder of medieval buildings. Sadly, there is no evidence of any meetings or correspondence between the two men, though Britton made journeys to Shrewsbury and Welshpool which are described in his autobiography of 1850.

When Britton was beginning his career as the compiler of *The Beauties of England and Wales*, there was intense debate about the origins of the pointed arch, the key feature of the Gothic style. Was it to be sought in England, France, Germany or even in Islamic countries? How did the style evolve, and where were the best examples to be found? Discussing such questions was made easier in 1812 when Thomas Rickman proposed that the architecture of the medieval period be considered in four phases: Norman, Early English, Decorated and Perpendicular, a taxonomy which is still followed. Parker was very much a disciple of Rickman, Britton and his fellow antiquarians; like them, he believed that the zenith of the Gothic style was the Decorated and he was reluctant to appreciate what we now see as the glories of the Perpendicular.

The rediscovery of medieval art and architecture, and the adoption of Gothic as the increasingly popular style for new buildings, did raise some problems for its advocates. The Reformation of the sixteenth-century was a disaster for Gothic architecture in Britain: the dissolution of the monasteries – the greatest act of vandalism in our history – and the iconoclasm which obliterated many monuments and much stained glass, was the work of the monarchs who created the Anglican state church. For Catholic antiquarians, and there were many, the revival of Gothic was a logical return to the days before the great disruption. For Anglicans, like Parker, this posed a quandary: the pre-Reformation churches were built for Catholic worship and, for most of the nineteenth-century, hostility to the Church of Rome was intense.

The revival of interest in Gothic architecture in Parker's lifetime was not unchallenged; the advocates of classical taste did not surrender meekly and the 'Battle of the Styles' raged over the design of many important buildings, including the new Foreign Office, well into the 1850s. This was a period of unprecedented building which would transform the appearance of Britain; new factories, warehouses, railway stations, town and city halls, schools, hospitals, asylums and churches were built in styles ranging from the Romanesque to the Egyptian. The most famous advocate of Gothic taste was A. W. N. Pugin and, in his book *Contrasts*, published in 1836, he argued for the moral superiority of the style. Parker needed no persuasion – in his view, Gothic *was* superior; he went further and believed 'no other style should be employed for churches and we are likely to see the gothic prevailing to the exclusion of all other styles in every department of public and private architecture.'[55] The two men shared a delight in medieval buildings and ornamentation as the decoration of the churches in Llanmyrewig and Llanyblodwel testifies. But Parker found Pugin problematic because in the year before *Contrasts* appeared he was received into the Catholic church. A visit to St Mary's Roman Catholic Church in Derby in 1851 gave Parker an opportunity to voice his doubts about Pugin. 'It is a consolation to see that Pugin the Romantist, after all his boasting cannot build a satisfactory church ... I disliked the slender slightness of the piers, the late gothic of the clerestory, the aisle windows out of all proportion, wide and filled with yellow glass, the effeminate weakness of the chancel vaulting.'[56]

The nineteenth-century building boom involved the provision of thousands of new churches. By 1820, it was clear that the steep increase and redistribution of the population had created problems for the Established Church. While Nonconformists were building chapels at a furious pace, Anglican provision was lamentable; many parish churches were in desperate need of repair and in the new industrial towns there were few, if any, Anglican churches. The government responded with a grant of a million pounds in 1818, followed by half million six years later. To these sums were added the contributions by the Incorporated Church Building Society and the generous donations by lay people of all classes.

The building of so many new churches sharpened the rivalry between the advocates of classical and Gothic styles. For Parker, a church *had* to be Gothic. 'Our gothic churches infinitely surpass all other displays of architectural talent ... Our wiser ancestors when they built their churches made it a point of so enriching the suspended vault that we should naturally be attracted by it, and led upward instead of being altogether cast upon the earth or wandering among the congregation.'[57]

While he made clear in his journals and other memoranda that he considered the Decorated style the apogee of Gothic architecture, when it came to rebuilding his own churches, his taste was more eclectic, not to say eccentric. He acted as both architect and project manager, although he did call on some engineering advice in the case of Llanmyrewig.[58] The work was largely paid for out of his own pocket.

At Llanmyrewig in 1827, he found a typical small, Welsh rural church with nave and chancel under one roof and a bell turret at the west end. By 1843, the church had acquired a new vestry with an Elizabethan chimney at the north-east corner, new windows in the nave, an elaborate porch and doorway, and the most incongruous Italian-style campanile as a bell tower. The transformation of the interior was, if anything, even more dramatic. Parker designed new ceilings for the nave and the vestry, a gallery at the west end, and an extraordinary pulpit and reading desk which would not have looked out of place in a cathedral. This certainly fulfilled his aim that the pulpit should be 'the place of exhortation more than of

Masonry for the new porch

prayer ... Let the preacher therefore have every possible advantage of situation that his looks and gestures as well as his voice may render the meaning clear to those who are farthest from him.'[59]

The progress of the work is indicated by datestones on the tower and the nave wall but also in scores of Parker's drawings and paintings, which make it one of the best recorded restorations of the nineteenth-century. It is fortunate that the rector was such an accomplished artist because all of his flamboyant interior was swept away in the 1890s.

In 1844, he left Montgomeryshire for his new living at Llanyblodwel, which, despite its name, is in Shropshire,

Parker's campanile

an area of the border that Parker knew well from his days at Sweeney Hall. Here again, he found a church, rather larger than Llanmyrewig, also in need of restoration. The challenge was an opportunity for Parker to further deploy his skills and enthusiasm for architectural display and decoration. As far as the body of the church was concerned, Parker's rebuilding is most obvious in the south wall of the nave, where a new porch was built and larger windows were inserted. Most visitors however would have already had their eyes fixed on the tower, which dominates the scene.

The tower is a hybrid, neither round nor square, surmounted by a tapering spire; it is quite unlike anything else in the country. Parker based his design on the minster church in Freiburg, which he visited on his European journey in 1827. In 'Suggestions and remarks as to the construction and improvement of churches', he advised that the tower should be 'such as the steeple at Friburg [sic] Germany where very tall clustered pinnacles rising from a square tower flank four sides of a smaller octagon upon which the spire itself rises.'[60] The pinnacles were not added at Llanyblodwel, but the unusual shape and proportions of the tower make a dramatic impression, particularly in a secluded, rural setting.

Inside the church, Parker showed more restraint than he did at Llanmyrewig. The stencilled patterns and inscriptions on the walls are the most obvious evidence of his work; he had noticed such decoration on his tour of the south of England in 1838, when he visited the Hospital of St Cross in Winchester. 'The whole interior of this church was originally covered with stencil patterns, painted on the stone. These not unlike modern paper [wallpaper] patterns, extended not merely over the flat surfaces of walls, but over the clustered columns and pier mouldings. One of them I copied. It exhibited a couple of red rods croped [sic] with buds at both ends ... the other ... apparently consisted of curling foliage.'[61] The altar and reredos were also Parker's work,

The new vestry

Llanmyrewig church interior after Parker's restoration

something of which, ironically, Pugin would have been proud. The ceilings are similar to those he installed at his new vicarage and earlier at Llanmyrewig church.

In fact, the house he built at Llanyblodwel was not in the Gothic style but in what is now described as Jacobethan, an amalgam of late sixteenth- and early seventeenth-century features. The entrance front is similar to the E-shaped houses of the later Tudor period, but with Dutch gables above the porch and the two wings. On the garden side, the fenestration and decoration is less regular and includes a three-light Early English window on the first floor. The house has a fine collection of the prominent brick chimneys with which Parker loved to ornament his buildings (the first appeared on the church at Llanmyrewig). The entrance to the garden was through a gate in a battlemented wall, with the inscription (in Gothic lettering) 'Salvation belongeth to the Lord'. Parker expended much care over the planting of the garden, which sloped down to the River Tanat.

Work on the vicarage was completed in 1853, but the remodelling of the church continued. In September 1856, Parker signed a conveyance for a parcel of land from Lord Bradford of Weston Park, on which he proposed building a new school and a schoolmaster's house. Sited about 400 yards west of the church, the two new buildings were designed to complement each other and to demonstrate his belief in the superiority of the Gothic style. Parker's school included some very personal features, including the remarkable gable-end chimney stack which augments the dramatic silhouette the building presents as approached from the church. Smaller – but with features more likely to grace a much larger building – is the schoolmaster's house, which Parker described as 'what I mean by a Gothic house'.[62]

At Llanyblodwel today, Parker's buildings are still prominent landmarks and regarded as important examples of Victorian taste. However, his contemporaries were not always complimentary. In the last year of his life, Parker was involved in an acrimonious correspondence in *The Builder*, the most influential architectural journal of the period.[63] On 3 December 1859, a letter signed M.R.I.B.A. (presumably standing for Member of the Royal Institute of British Architects) objected to the proposal 'to elect the Rev. John Parker, of Llanyblodwell, [sic] near Oswestry, as honorary member'. In the writer's opinion, 'I never saw or imagined greater abortions of architectural science … than have been the result of the genius of this same Mr John Parker.' He has 'built a spire to his church and if originality be a work of genius, such originality deserves a statue to Mr. Parker in Westminster Abbey; for there is nothing in Heaven or earth, or in the waters under the earth like it'. His opinion of Parker's school was no less scathing. 'Gothic, I suppose of the reign of Semiramis … it has no semblance to buildings of its usual class', having buttresses 'strong enough to support Salisbury spire'. 'Let people be amateur architects as much as they like on paper, but not put up abortions to disgust the public.'

Parker responded to this attack in a letter of January

Llanmyrewig church, date on the tower

Llanyblodwel church before restoration, Edward Williams, 1790 by permission of Shropshire Archives

Llanyblodwel church after Parker's restoration

New window dated 1847

Llanyblodwel church from the north-west

7th 1860. He expressed surprise that his critic was unaware of the example of 'Fribourg minster, in Germany' on which he based his tower at the church. The school and master's house he was proud to acknowledge as being 'unlike the ordinary type of national schools in other places' and the Gothic 'I consider our own appropriate living style, ductile beyond all others'. Parker objected to the 'professional exclusiveness of architects who were happy to provide ground plan, elevation and working drawings &, [but] will hardly visit the spot more frequently than twice in a twelvemonth', whereas Parker was present on site

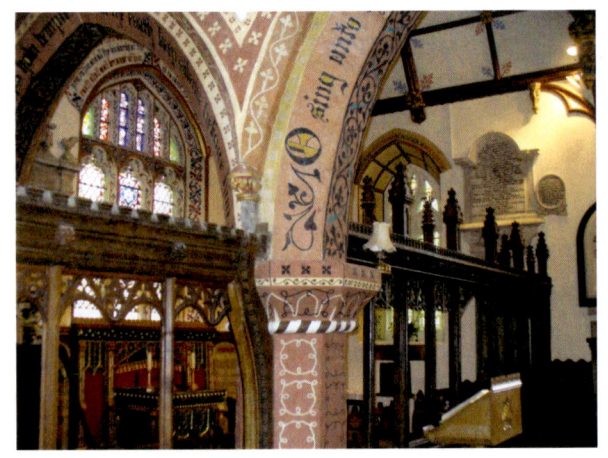

Llanyblodwel church Parker's decoration

Llanyblodwel Old Vicarage, garden gate

Llanyblodwel church nave ceiling

Llanyblodwel Old Vicarage

almost every day to personally supervise the building work. 'Never until now, that I am aware of, has it been made a matter of reproach to a clergyman, that he has turned his attention to architecture, as a branch of knowledge connected with his profession.'

At a meeting of the R.I.B.A. in December 1859 (after the publication of the letter in *The Builder* attacking Parker), it was proposed that he be elected an honorary fellow of the Institute. His proposer, who is not named, cited Parker's 'knowledge of architecture, and his merits as a draughtsman' in support of his election. The matter was discussed and 'Mr. Scott' [George Gilbert Scott]

The Old Vicarage, dated window

Interior of schoolmaster's house

'N.E. view of Blodwell school and Master's house J.P. 1859'

Llanyblodwel school and schoolmaster's house today

'said he had personal knowledge of the Rev. Mr. Parker, and that the rev. gentleman had devoted the best part of his life and all his energies to old English architecture'. However, Scott 'did not know whether he had produced any work on the subject'. Despite Scott's recommendation, the R.I.B.A. council postponed a decision on Parker's election, which might be brought forward 'at a future day'. Although denied recognition by the R.I.B.A., the testimony of Scott, the most successful architect of his day, is an honour in itself and further proof of the esteem in which Parker was held.

[52] In Hill, *op.cit.*, 32, the author describes the how 'the antiquary's interests were shared by poets and novelists ... and architects, as well as readers and tourists of the polite, middling classes'.

[53] *Gentleman's Magazine,* 209 July to December 1860, 675–78.

[54] John Britton, J. Mordaunt Crook, *Oxford Dictionary of National Biography* (2008), accessed 6 August 2021.

[55] NLW MS 19382E, 8, 'On Gothic art'.

[56] NLW MS 16089C, 'Journal 1851, Midland Counties'.

[57] NLW MS. 18254B, '*Journal of a Gothic Tour to Winchester, Salisbury, & Bristol 1838*'.

[58] Edward Parry, *op. cit.*

[59] NLW MS 19382E, 7.

[60] '*Ibid*'.

[61] NLW MS. 18254B, '*Journal of a Gothic Tour to Winchester, Salisbury, & Bristol 1838*'.

[62] Shropshire Archives, Sweeney Hall Miscellany X7634, Box 1, 2 March 1859.

[63] The correspondence and subsequent discussions about Parker's election to the R.I.B.A. in *The Builder* can be read online.

Conclusion

Unlike most of the travellers whose published works influenced how Wales and its inhabitants were perceived outside the country, Parker lived in Wales or very close to the Welsh border all his life. Wherever he travelled, Parker compared his surroundings to Wales, always to its advantage. What Parker saw when he drew the mountains of North Wales was influenced by his Romantic version of Welsh history. Wales was 'the land of Druidic, Bardic and Feudal glory', but also a country of misfortune, conquest and subjection. Caractacus, Arthur, the Druids, the princes of Gwynedd and their bards fought against invaders, whether Roman, Saxon or English. Such a past gave Snowdonia its unique appeal.

In one of his notebooks, when practising his Gothic calligraphy, he ascribed to 'Cambrian elders' the laws and customs valued by his contemporaries:

Whence come those customs, those laws, henceforth to be valued As the precious birthright of a nation? Not from Italian Craftiness; or the caverns of Germany; but from a western Tribe; from a Celtic land: from you ye Cambrian elders!

Parker deserves to be remembered as one of Wales's greatest friends and admirers, for whom Snowdonia was his emotional homeland and to which he returned continually for inspiration and reassurance. An English gentleman, a bachelor clergyman, he left a legacy of paintings and writings which are unsurpassed as a record of the beauties of North Wales.

At the end of his tour of Snowdonia in 1820 he wrote, 'We have seen lands pregnant with magnificent records of History and the last residence of the Bardic institution ... where else could our time have been employed more pleasingly or where with more advantage or more profit?'

John Parker's monument in Llanyblodwel churchyard

Postscript

SNOWDONIA, THE MARY AND FRANCES LEIGHTON TRIBUTE TO PARKER

In 1835, Mary Leighton created a memorial to her elder brother Thomas, who died in 1833. Mary transcribed Thomas's journals and copied drawings he made of his journey to the Crimea. The result, over 500 pages in three volumes, in now at the Yale Center for British Art.[64]

When John died, Mary embarked on a similar literary and artistic memorial. The result, a handsome volume bound in green morocco, was presented to the National Library in August 1946 by Mrs Alfred Sotheby (Catherina Barbara Leighton), Parker's great-niece. Included in the book are a family tree (compiled in the 1930s), obituary notices from the Gentlemen's Magazine and Archaeologia Cambrensis, and a photograph of the Halle portrait of Parker.[65]

The volume brings together all the enthusiasms and interests which John Parker pursued throughout his life. There is a selection of paintings, showing the two churches he transformed, the vicarage at Llanyblodwel (with the garden he created below the house to the river) and the new school at Llanyblodwel. Most of these are copies of Parker's paintings by Mary's daughter Frances, one is by Mary, and two – the best – are originals.

Parker's poem 'Snowdonia' is the centrepiece of the book, with an extensive commentary by the author. He describes the poem as 'a specimen of a thoroughly Gothic and romantic poem grounded nonetheless on strict adherence to the rules of the Greek metres', thus combining his love of classical literature with nineteenth-century sensibilities. Parker was a much better artist and prose writer than poet. 'Snowdonia', while a testament to his deep love of and reverence for the landscape, often descends into mawkish sentimentality.

The poem is similar in content to 'The Celtic Annals' and portrays Wales as a land of bards, warriors and heroes. The verses are set out as an illuminated manuscript, with Gothic lettering and marginal decorations, in a Celtic style; Parker's notebooks contain many examples of just this type of script, which shows where Mary found her inspiration. Each verse is accompanied by two painted scenes, a smaller one in the top left-hand corner (where the initial letter of an illuminated manuscript would be), showing either an historic building or a mountain scene, and a larger one below the verse with a scene in Snowdonia. Buildings are represented by the castles at Conwy and Dolbadarn, Beddgelert church and a view of Cologne cathedral. However, the majority of the illustrations are views of Snowdon and its nearby peaks, Crib Goch and Y Lliwedd, reflecting the admiration and awe with which Parker viewed them throughout his life.

Frances Leighton, *Blodwel Vicarage on the banks of the Tanat*

[64] Y.C.B.A., Mary Leighton collection, 1824–1860.
[65] NLW, Mary Leighton, *Snowdonia,* Drawing Volume 352.

Mary Leighton, *Dolbadarn Castle and Llyn Gwynant*

Mary Leighton, *Choir of Cologne and Snowdon from the summit of Glydar Vach*

Acknowledgements

The generous deposit by the Parker-Leighton family of hundreds of Parker's paintings, sketches and drawings and later of his travel journals made this book possible. At the library the staff were unfailingly helpful in responding to requests for Parker material; the patient assistance of Emyr Evans in arranging for the reproduction of the illustrations from the collection was invaluable. I am also grateful to the staff at Shropshire archives and Oswestry Town Council archives for their help.

At Loton Park Sir Michael Leighton Bt kindly showed me items associated with Parker. The owners of Parker's three Llanyblodwel buildings – Mr and Mrs Shellard at Woodland House (the Old Vicarage), Mr and Mrs Lloyd at the Old School and Mr and Mrs Gordon at the Old School House – allowed me unlimited access to their homes and shared my enthusiasm for their architect.

Melvin Humphreys gave me his notes for a lecture on Parker and encouraged me to undertake further research. Tom Lloyd offered advice on Gentry Houses. Professor Malcolm Airs read various early drafts of the text and suggested significant improvements. The two readers for the The Books Council of Wales made detailed comments and constructive criticisms of a later draft and I have adopted many of their suggested changes to the organisation of the book. For advice and guidance on placing Parker among the landscape painters of Snowdonia I am grateful to Peter Bishop who generously shared his expertise as both artist and author. Michael Freeman's website, *Early Tourists in Wales, 18th and 19th century tourists' comments about Wales*, is an incomparable source for material about Wales at the time of Parker's visits. During the writing of this book I have plundered the website for references as well as bombarding Michael with questions which he always answered promptly and comprehensively.

Myrddin ap Dafydd of Gwasg Carreg Gwalch took the brave decision to accept a rough draft from an unknown author – in very uncertain times – and see it through to publication. Dwynwen S. Williams was an eagle-eyed typesetter and Eleri Owen supervised the book's elegant design.

Index

Aberllefenni 98
Aberystwyth 26
Aneirin 58
Anglesey 45, 69, 88
Anglesey Column 101
Arans/Arrans 59, 64
Bangor 26, 44, 46, 48, 51, 52, 57, 88, 92, 93, 94
Barmouth 20, 22, 56, 64, 76, 80
Beaumaris 49, 50, 51, 88, 94, 95, 96
Beddgelert 38, 48, 49, 56, 57, 116
Betws-y-coed 46, 48, 52, 57, 66, 87, 100
Bodowen 15, 20, 56, 64, 65, 66, 90, 97
Britton, John 38, 106
Caernarfon/Carnarvon 25, 37, 42, 50, 56, 94, 95
Calvinistic Methodists 25, 59
Cambrian Archaeological Association 23, 86, 97
Capel Curig 22, 32, 44, 45, 46, 48, 49, 50, 52, 56, 76, 100
Clanvoy (Parker) 30, 31
Clynnog Fawr 59, 92
Cnicht 59, 64, 78, 79
Cockney 51, 100
Conwy/Conway 44, 45, 49, 59, 63, 89, 90, 92, 94, 95, 96, 100, 116
Corwen 46, 48, 64, 76
Cwm Dyli 55, 58, 59
Dolbadarn 52, 57, 69, 116, 117
Druids 50, 115
Eryri/Snowdonia 9, 15, 23, 30, 32, 36, 38, 41, 42, 44, 45, 46, 48, 49, 50, 52, 56, 57, 58, 59, 62, 63, 66, 67, 68, 76, 78, 87, 94, 115, 118
Eton 12, 13, 14, 15, 41, 42, 74, 75, 79
Evan Jones 32, 50
Freeman, Michael 37, 50, 118
Gilpin, William 36, 38
Glyderau/ the Glyders 56, 68
Griffith, Moses 38, 77
Holyhead 45, 46, 47, 48, 69
Hotels 46, 48, 50, 52, 56
Irish Road 32, 44, 45, 46, 56, 99
Ladies of Llangollen 46, 48, 74
Lake District 36, 57, 66, 67

Leighton, Catherina Barbara 116
Leighton, Frances 116
Leighton, Sir Baldwin Bt 12
Llananno 9, 90
Llanbedrog 56
Llanberis 25, 26, 44, 46, 48, 50, 52, 56, 57, 59, 68, 69, 76, 77
Llanengan 50, 92, 93, 94
Llangollen 45, 46, 47, 48, 67, 74, 86, 87
Llangurig 25
Llanmyrewig 15, 20, 22, 42, 45, 58, 80, 94, 107, 109, 109, 110
Llanrwst 44, 45, 50, 60, 87, 90, 91, 93, 94, 98
Llanyblodwel/Blodwel 12, 20, 22, 24, 42, 44, 56, 66, 70, 80, 107, 108, 109, 110, 111,112, 113, 115, 116, 118
Lliwedd 56, 116
Llyn Geirionydd 57, 58, 66, 77
Llyn peninsula 44, 64, 92
Llyn Tegid/ Bala Lake 38
Llyn-y-Gader 41
Luxmoore Charles (Cory) 12, 13, 56
Luxmoore John (Bishop) 12, 20, 91
Maen Du/Poetmaking Stone 29, 32, 68, 78
Menai Bridge 100
Menai Straits 48, 49, 69, 100
Moel Siabod 15, 42, 50, 56, 63
Moreton 20
Nonconformity 23, 25, 26, 107
Ogwen Falls 56
Oriel College 13, 15, 16
Oswestry 12, 20, 22, 30, 45, 46, 47, 52, 57, 67, 99, 110, 118
Parker, Thomas 12, 74, 75, 116
Parker, Elizabeth 12, 56
Parker, Mary (Lady Leighton) 9, 12, 15, 46, 56, 74, 75, 116, 117
Parker, Thomas Netherton 12
Pen y Gwryd 49, 50
Penarth 22, 45 70
Pennant, Melangell 44
Pennant, Thomas 37, 38, 77
Penrhyn Arms 48, 51, 52
Penrhyn Castle 100, 101

Picturesque, the 32, 35, 36, 37, 39, 77, 96
Pistyll Rhaeadr 66
Pistyll Blaen Cwm 66
Plas Newydd (Llangollen) 46
Pwllheli 56, 58, 92
Rhineland 9, 15, 30
Ruthven, John 57
Sedgwick, Professor 57, 68
Shrewsbury 45, 74, 75, 99, 101, 106
Snowdonia, memorial volume 116
St Asaph 12, 13, 20, 44, 56
Sweeney Hall 11, 12, 15, 20, 45, 66, 109
Taliesin 58
Telford, Thomas 45, 49, 99, 100
The Passengers 9, 29, 30, 32, 38, 50, 56, 58, 59, 86, 87, 90, 99, 106
Valle Crucis 44, 86, 87
Warner, Rev. Richard 38
Welsh language 25, 26, 58, 59
Yr Wyddfa/ Snowdon 9, 25, 30, 32, 35, 37, 38, 39, 41, 42, 44, 45, 46, 48, 56, 57, 59, 61, 63, 64, 66, 68, 69, 70, 76, 77, 116